**At Issue**

| Student Loans

# Other Books in the At Issue Series:

# At Issue

# I Student Loans

*Dedria Bryfonski, Book Editor*

**GREENHAVEN PRESS**
*A part of Gale, Cengage Learning*

Detroit • New York • San Francisco • New Haven, Conn • Waterville, Maine • London

Elizabeth Des Chenes, *Managing Editor*

© 2012 Greenhaven Press, a part of Gale, Cengage Learning.

Gale and Greenhaven Press are registered trademarks used herein under license.

*For more information, contact:*
Greenhaven Press
27500 Drake Rd.
Farmington Hills, MI 48331-3535
Or you can visit our Internet site at gale.cengage.com

For product information and technology assistance, contact us at

Gale Customer Support, 1-800-877-4253
For permission to use material from this text or product, submit all requests online at www.cengage.com/permissions.

Further permissions questions can be e-mailed to permissionrequest@cengage.com.

Articles in Greenhaven Press anthologies are often edited for length to meet page requirements. In addition, original titles of these works are changed to clearly present the main thesis and to explicitly indicate the author's opinion. Every effort is made to ensure that Greenhaven Press accurately reflects the original intent of the authors. Every effort has been made to trace the owners of copyrighted material.

Cover image copyright © Todd Davidson/Illustration Works/Corbis.

**LIBRARY OF CONGRESS CATALOGING-IN-PUBLICATION DATA**

Student loans / Dedria Bryfonski, book editor.
    p. cm. -- (At issue)
  Includes bibliographical references and index.
  ISBN 978-0-7377-5600-5 (hardcover) -- ISBN 978-0-7377-5601-2 (pbk.)
  1. Student loans--United States--Juvenile literature. 2. Student loans--Government policy--United States--Juvenile literature. I. Bryfonski, Dedria.
  LB2340.2.S846 2012
  371.2'240973--dc23
                         2011030832

Printed in the United States of America
1 2 3 4 5 6 7 15 14 13 12 11

# Contents

# Introduction

Today's controversies surrounding the financing of higher education in the United States have deep roots. The founding fathers of the country were conflicted about the role of the federal government in providing funding for higher education. Some delegates to the Constitutional Convention of 1787, notably Thomas Jefferson and James Madison, believed a democracy needs an educated citizenry and pushed for a national university. Their efforts were unsuccessful, as it was deemed that education was a matter best left to the states. Thus, for the next century and a half, access to higher education was largely limited to those who could afford to pay for it—predominately white, Protestant males from the upper classes of society. Prior to World War II, only 5 percent of the population over the age of twenty-five had an undergraduate degree.

That landscape changed abruptly in the years following the Second World War and the passing of the Serviceman's Readjustment Act of 1944, which became known as the GI Bill. The GI Bill provided funding for up to three years of college for men and women who had served for at least two years in the military. Of the 16 million veterans serving in World War II, 7.8 million received training or education covered by the GI Bill. In 1947, veterans made up 49 percent of all college students. An updated version of the GI Bill passed in 1966 to help Vietnam-era veterans provided educational aid for an additional 7 million servicemen and servicewomen. Most of these veterans were from middle-class and lower-class families and would have been unable to afford college without assistance. It is important to note that these funds were not loans requiring repayment but were considered part of the compensation due veterans for service to their country.

The next defining event for student aid occurred on October 4, 1957, when the Soviet Union launched Sputnik I into space, setting off the space race. The US government feared its citizens would lag behind the Soviets in the key areas of science and engineering, and in 1958 the National Defense Education Act was passed, which provided direct student loans at a 5 percent interest rate. In later years, these loans became known as Perkins Loans, named after a US representative from Kentucky, Carl D. Perkins. Perkins Loans were direct loans from the federal government to the student. In "The Kids Aren't Alright: The Policymaking of Student Loan Debt," published in the journal *Origins*, economic historian Lawrence Bowdish writes:

> Ensuring that all people can afford a college education is important. It offers a degree of social justice, ensures that talented individuals can excel despite their socioeconomic background, and allows the country to remain competitive in a global economy that increasingly requires trained and talented workers. During the 20th century, and especially during the Cold War, the U.S. focused on producing an educated population in its efforts to lead the world and outperform the Soviet Union.

In 1965, the federal government passed the Higher Education Act, which established Stafford Loans under the Federal Family Education Loan (FFEL) program. Unlike Perkins Loans, Stafford Loans were not direct to the student but provided in partnership with private enterprise. Under a Stafford Loan, the government essentially guaranteed to the lender that the loan would be repaid and encouraged students to take out loans by its underwriting of a portion of the interest payment once the student graduated.

With the reauthorization of the Higher Education Act in 1972, the Student Loan Marketing Association (Sallie Mae) was created to service government-guaranteed student loans. Sallie Mae was privatized in 2004. Also part of the reauthorization was the creation of the Basic Education Opportunity Grant, which provided educational grants to low-income students. Renamed Pell Grants in 1980 in honor of Rhode Island Senator Claiborne Pell, who was instrumental in their development, these grants in 2011 provide up to fifty-five hundred dollars a year to qualifying students.

From 1972 to the present time, politicians have debated the virtues of direct loans versus guaranteed loans, essentially with most Republican lawmakers backing guaranteed loans and most Democrat lawmakers preferring direct loans. During most of this time, both approaches were used, with direct lending on a decline until 2008. The credit crisis that began in 2008 caused many private lenders to stop making student loans. The 2010 Student Loan Bill was signed into law on March 30, 2010, essentially eliminating the FFEL program with its guarantees and replacing it with the Federal Direct Loan Program (FDLP), which makes loans directly to the student or parent. Although guaranteed student loans with their subsidies to private lenders have been eliminated, the debate continues as to the best way to fund higher education.

According to Robert B. Archibald in *Redesigning the Financial Aid System: Why Colleges and Universities Should Switch Roles with the Federal Government*:

> The financial aid system of today resembles something that has been patched up many times with duct tape, baling wire, clothespins, and spit. It is dizzyingly complex, and it is not doing its job efficiently. Many students who should take advantage of the financial aid system are unable to do so, and often the students who do receive financial aid receive less aid than they need. A thoroughgoing redesign of the financial aid system is in order.

Opinions abound on what to do about student loans, but most agree with Archibald's statement that change is needed. In the viewpoints that follow, journalists, economists, analysts, and commentators debate such topics as the value of Pell

Grants, the role of for-profit colleges, whether or not student loan debt should be forgiven, and whether student loan debt is toxic or good debt.

# 1

# Federally Guaranteed Student Loans Are Good Debt

*Sandra Block*

*Sandra Block reports on personal finance for the daily national newspaper* USA Today.

*The debt taken out for student loans is considered good debt, because the average graduate of a four-year college earns 62 percent more than someone with just a high school diploma. However, there are different types of loans. Stafford loans, which are guaranteed by the federal government, have lower interest rates and offer other protections.*

In the Land of Oz, there are good witches and bad witches. Likewise, in the land of borrowing, there's good debt and bad debt. A home mortgage? Good debt, because the interest is tax-deductible, your home will likely rise in value over time, and you'll have a roof over your head. A credit card loan to buy a pair of designer sandals? Bad debt, because credit card interest isn't deductible, your purchase will decline in value and you can't live in your shoes.

## Not All Student Loans Are Alike

Student loans are often categorized as good debt, because a college education is considered a sensible long-term investment. In 2005, the typical full-time worker with a four-year college degree earned 62% more than an employee with only a high school diploma, according to the College Board. And many students can't afford to attend college without borrowing money.

But it's important to understand that not all student loans are alike. Federally guaranteed student loans, known as Stafford loans, have fixed interest rates, now [in 2007] 6.8%, and flexible repayment terms. Any full-time college student, regardless of family income, can take out a Stafford loan.

Private student loans, which are often offered by the same lenders that provide federal loans, are more expensive. Interest rates are variable, so there's no limit on how high they can go. And repayment terms aren't as flexible as they are for federal loans.

Yet despite these drawbacks, private student loan borrowing has soared in the past decade. This year [2007], private loans accounted for 29% of all loans taken out by undergraduates, according to a report released last week by the College Board.

The amount of federal money that students can borrow is limited, and those limits haven't kept up with increases in college costs. As a result, some students who attend high-cost schools rely on private loans to pay for expenses not covered by their federal loans.

But that doesn't entirely explain the growth in private loans. An analysis by the American Council on Education found that one in five undergraduates with private loans didn't first take full advantage of federal loans.

---

*Federal loans are much cheaper and have many more protections.*

---

So why do borrowers take out higher-cost loans? Marketing probably plays a role. Many lenders advertise private loans on television and over the Internet. The U.S. Public Interest Research Group, a consumer advocacy group, has charged that some of these ads are misleading and entice borrowers to take out unnecessarily high-risk, high-cost loans. Last month [September 2007], New York Attorney General Andrew Cuomo expanded his investigation of the student-loan industry to include lenders and companies that use direct-marketing campaigns to promote their loans. (Major private lenders say they encourage borrowers to take advantage of federal loans before taking out any private loans.)

In addition, recent cuts in government subsidies have made federal loans less profitable for lenders. Consequently, lenders may become even more aggressive in marketing their private loans, says Stephen Burd, senior research fellow for the New America Foundation, a policy institute.

## Federal Loans Are Superior to Private

Ads for private loans often point out that borrowers don't have to start repaying the loans until six months after graduation. But what they fail to mention is that this feature isn't unique to private loans. Repayments on federal student loans, too, are deferred until six months after graduation.

Many ads for private loans also claim that loan applicants can get their money in less than a week. By contrast, Stafford loan borrowers must fill out a Free Application for Federal Student Aid [FAFSA], which is eight pages long and contains more than 100 questions.

But while the FAFSA takes time, it's time well spent. Congress recently added some important benefits to the federal student loan program. Under a $20 billion financial aid bill enacted last month [September 2007], Stafford loan borrowers will never have to spend more than 15% of their discretionary income on loan payments.

The law also gradually reduces interest rates over the next four years for new federally subsidized Stafford loans, which are available to borrowers who can show financial need. The government pays the interest on subsidized Stafford loans while the borrower is in school.

In addition, borrowers who work in certain public-service jobs for at least 10 years will be eligible to have the balance of their student loans forgiven. But this relief will be available only to borrowers with federal loans.

"There seems to be no reason for students to take out private loans without exhausting their federal eligibility first," Burd notes. "Federal loans are much cheaper and have many more protections."

# 2

# Student Loans Are Toxic Debt

*Mary Pilon*

*Mary Pilon is a journalist who writes about money matters for the* Wall Street Journal.

*Although student loan debt is often termed "good debt," in reality it can be an extremely dangerous financial burden. Student loans are not forgiven in bankruptcy proceedings, and thus they are very difficult to get out of. Additionally, once a borrower defaults on a loan, interest compounds, and collection fees are added. Sometimes, the obligation is triple that of the original loan.*

When Michelle Bisutti, a 41-year-old family practitioner in Columbus, Ohio, finished medical school in 2003, her student-loan debt amounted to roughly $250,000. Since then, it has ballooned to $555,000.

It is the result of her deferring loan payments while she completed her residency, default charges and relentlessly compounding interest rates. Among the charges: a single $53,870 fee for when her loan was turned over to a collection agency.

"Maybe half of it was my fault because I didn't look at the fine print," Dr. Bisutti says. "But this is just outrageous now."

## Student Loans Are Hard to Get Out Of

To be sure, Dr. Bisutti's case is extreme, and lenders say student-loan terms are clear and that they try to work with borrowers who get in trouble.

But as tuitions rise, many people are borrowing heavily to pay their bills. Some no doubt view it as "good debt," because an education can lead to a higher salary. But in practice, student loans are one of the most toxic debts, requiring extreme consumer caution and, as Dr. Bisutti learned, responsibility.

Unlike other kinds of debt, student loans can be particularly hard to wriggle out of. Homeowners who can't make their mortgage payments can hand over the keys to their house to their lender. Credit-card and even gambling debts can be discharged in bankruptcy. But ditching a student loan is virtually impossible, especially once a collection agency gets involved. Although lenders may trim payments, getting fees or principals waived seldom happens.

---

*Student loans are one of the most toxic debts, requiring extreme consumer caution and . . . responsibility.*

---

Yet many former students are trying. There is an estimated $730 billion in outstanding federal and private student-loan debt, says Mark Kantrowitz of FinAid.org, a Web site that tracks financial-aid issues—and only 40% of that debt is actively being repaid. The rest is in default, or in deferment, which means that payments and interest are halted, or in "forbearance," which means payments are halted while interest accrues.

Although Dr. Bisutti's debt load is unusual, her experience having problems repaying isn't. Emmanuel Tellez's mother is a laid-off factory worker, and $120 from her $300 unemployment checks is garnished to pay the federal PLUS student loan she took out for her son.

By the time Mr. Tellez graduated in 2008, he had $50,000 of his own debt in loans issued by SLM Corp., known as Sallie Mae, the largest private student lender. In December, he was laid off from his $29,000-a-year job in Boston and defaulted. Mr. Tellez says that when he signed up, the loan wasn't explained to him well, though he concedes he missed the fine print.

Loan terms, including interest rates, are disclosed "multiple times and in multiple ways," says Martha Holler, a spokeswoman for Sallie Mae, who says the company can't comment on individual accounts. Repayment tools and account information are accessible on Sallie Mae's Web site as well, she says.

---

*There is an estimated $730 billion in outstanding federal and private student-loan debt . . . and only 40% of that debt is actively being repaid.*

---

## The Terms of Loans Are Difficult to Adjust

Many borrowers say they are experiencing difficulties working out repayment and modification terms on their loans. Ms. Holler says that Sallie Mae works with borrowers individually to revamp loans. Although the U.S. Department of Education has expanded programs like income-based repayment, which effectively caps repayments for some borrowers, others might not qualify.

Heather Ehmke of Oakland, Calif., renegotiated the terms of her subprime mortgage after her home was foreclosed. But even after filing for bankruptcy, she says she couldn't get Sallie Mae, one of her lenders, to adjust the terms on her student loan. After 14 years with patches of deferment and forbearance, the loan has increased from $28,000 to more than $90,000. Her monthly payments jumped from $230 to $816. Last month, her petition for undue hardship on the loans was dismissed.

Sallie Mae supports reforms that would allow student loans to be dischargeable in bankruptcy for those who have made a good-faith effort to repay them, says Ms. Holler.

Dr. Bisutti says she loves her work, but regrets taking out so many student loans. She admits that she made mistakes in missing payments, deferring her loans and not being completely thorough with some of the paperwork, but was surprised at how quickly the debt spiraled.

She says she knew when she started medical school in 1999 that she would have to borrow heavily. But she reasoned that her future income as a doctor would make paying off the loans easy. While in school, her loans racked up interest with variable rates ranging from 3% to 11%.

She maxed out on federal loans, borrowing $152,000 over four years, and sought private loans from Sallie Mae to help make up the difference. She also took out two loans from Wells Fargo & Co. for $20,000 each. Each had a $2,000 origination fee. The total amount she borrowed at the time: $250,000.

## Defaulters Are Subject to Harassment

In 2005, the bill for the Wells Fargo loans came due. Representatives from the bank called her father, Michael Bisutti, every day for two months demanding payment. Mr. Bisutti, who had co-signed on the loans, finally decided to cover the $550 monthly payments for a year.

Wells Fargo says it will stop calling consumers if they request it, says senior vice president Glen Herrick, who adds that the bank no longer imposes origination fees on its private loans.

Sallie Mae, meanwhile, called Mr. Bisutti's neighbor. The neighbor told Mr. Bisutti about the call. "Now they know [my dad's] daughter the doctor defaulted on her loans," Dr. Bisutti says.

Ms. Holler, the Sallie Mae spokeswoman, says that the company may contact a neighbor to verify an individual's address. But in those cases, she says, the details of the debt obligation aren't discussed.

Dr. Bisutti declined to authorize Sallie Mae to comment specifically on her case. "The overwhelming majority of medical-school graduates successfully repay their student loans," Ms. Holler says.

After completing her fellowship in 2007, Dr. Bisutti juggled other debts, including her credit-card balance, and was having trouble making her $1,000-a-month student-loan payments.

That year, she defaulted on both her federal and private loans. That is when the "collection cost" fee of $53,870 was added on to her private loan.

## Defaults Can Triple the Original Loan

Meanwhile, the variable interest rates continue to compound on her balance and fees. She recently applied for income-based repayment, but she still isn't sure if she will qualify. She makes $550-a-month payments to Wells Fargo for the two loans she hasn't defaulted on. By the time she is done, she will have paid the bank $128,000—over three times the $36,000 she received.

She recently entered a rehabilitation agreement on her defaulted federal loans, which now carry an additional $31,942 collection cost. She makes monthly payments on those loans—now $209,399—for $990 a month, with only $100 of it going toward her original balance. The entire balance of her federal loans will be paid off in 351 months. Dr. Bisutti will be 70 years old.

The debt load keeps her up at night. Her damaged credit has prevented her from buying a home or a new car. She says she and her boyfriend of three years have put off marriage and having children because of the debt.

Dr. Bisutti told her 17-year-old niece the story of her debt as a cautionary tale "so the next generation of kids who want to get a higher education knows what they're getting into," she says. "I will likely have to deal with this debt for the rest of my life."

# 3

# Student Loans Lack Consumer Protections

*Alan Collinge*

*Alan Collinge, a writer and political activist, is the founder of StudentLoanJustice.org, an organization that aims to improve consumer protection for student loans.*

*Student loans have fewer consumer protections than any other loans. Two-thirds of all students require loans to complete college, and the average student loan debt is more than twenty thousand dollars. Federal legislation has stripped basic consumer protection from student loans and made loans highly profitable for the student loan industry. Amendments to the Higher Education Act stipulated that student loans cannot be discharged in a bankruptcy, eliminated the statute of limitations for student loans, and added excessive penalties and fees for delinquent loans. The current system penalizes students and enriches lenders and needs to be changed.*

The halcyon days of higher education in the early 1970s, when the typical high school graduate could put him- or herself through college for a few thousand dollars (at most) in student loan debt and be able to repay this debt by working over the summers, are long gone. Today, about two-thirds of college students require loans to make it through, and the typical undergraduate borrower leaves school with more than twenty thousand dollars in student loan debt. For graduate

Alan Collinge, *The Student Loan Scam: The Most Oppressive Debt in US History—and How We Can Fight Back*. Boston: Beacon Press, 2008, pp. 1–21. Copyright © 2009 by Beacon Press. Reproduced by permission.

students, that amount more than doubles, to forty-two thousand dollars. Tuition inflation has outpaced the consumer price index (CPI) during this time period by a factor of about two to one.

## The New Reality

Also during this period, the Higher Education Act was amended six times, becoming progressively more lucrative for the lenders and less beneficial for the students. Over time, legislators gave more support to the interests of the student loan companies and the federal government than to the interests of the students. Bankruptcy protections, statutes of limitations, refinancing rights, and many other standard consumer protections vanished for student loans—and only for student loans. Concurrently, draconian collection tools were legislated into existence, and they provided unprecedented and unrivaled collection powers to the loan industry, including giving it the ability to garnish [seize] a borrower's wages, tax returns, Social Security, and disability income—all without a court order. Today, the student loan is an inescapable and profitable debt instrument unlike any other.

This lack of consumer protections has proven to be extremely beneficial for student loan companies, which were already guaranteed repayment of nearly the full unpaid balance of the loans in case of default. Student loan companies now realize extreme profits, not only because they collect interest on the loans from borrowers and special allowance (subsidy) payments from the federal government, but also because they collect penalties and fees on defaulted debt from the students who encountered financial difficulties repaying the original loans. Defaulted student loan debt with penalties, fees, collection charges, and compounded interest can double or triple the original balance—or worse. [Consumer advocate] Ralph Nader wrote in 2006 that "the corporate lawyers who conceived this self-enriching system ought to get the nation's top prize for shameless perversity." . . .

## The Rise of Sallie Mae

It is impossible to discuss the explosive growth of the student loan industry without examining the evolution of Sallie Mae [the Student Loan Marketing Association] from a government-sponsored entity to the dominant for-profit corporation in the business. . . .

The creation of Sallie Mae signaled the continuation and expansion of a trend that had begun with the passage of the Higher Education Act of 1965: namely, shifting the financial burden of attending college from the government to the students. . . .

Sallie Mae was not satisfied with being merely a student lender. The company wanted control of all aspects of the student loan industry: loans, guaranties, and collections. Thus began a monopolistic, acquisitional crusade by Sallie Mae. . . .

By 2006, Sallie Mae virtually dominated the student loan industry. It was about four times larger than its nearest competitor (Citibank), managed $123 billion in student loans, and by Wall Street's standards had become a stock-market rock star. It was now the largest player in all three parts of the student loan industry: loans, guaranties, and collections.

Notably, Sallie Mae had also become the nation's largest provider of *private* student loans. Such private loans, which are not guaranteed by the federal government, now account for 20 percent of all student loans and are extremely profitable for the lenders; although there are no federal subsidies for the loans, they typically carry with them interest rates far exceeding those of federally guaranteed loans. Interest rates of 18 percent or higher are not uncommon in the industry, and the national average interest rate is approximately 12 percent. Sallie Mae has been found to charge APRs [annual percentage rates] of as high as 28 percent.

Thus far, Sallie Mae's rise may appear to be a typical success story in American enterprise. After all, those companies that provide better products or services to their customers should succeed and thrive.... [However,] Sallie Mae was *not* a better company providing a better product or service to its customers. Rather, it was a politically sophisticated corporation that lobbied its way to extreme profitability at the expense of students and taxpayers. It used an unfair advantage bestowed on it by Congress to take over the industry and extract vast sums of unearned capital from misfortunate borrowers.

---

*By 2006, student loans had fewer consumer protections than any other type of loan instrument in the nation's history.*

---

## The Fall of Consumer Protections

In the 1990s, the new, privatized Sallie Mae gained control over the industry, and it used its power on Capitol Hill to great effect, convincing Congress to strip away nearly all consumer protections from student loans. It also lobbied for— and got—legislation that allowed for massive penalties and fees for delinquent debt, legislation that actually made it more profitable for the lenders and guarantors when students defaulted than when they paid. Senator Ted Kennedy, who was minority leader of the Senate Education Committee until 2007, when he became majority leader, remarked before an Education Committee meeting in the spring of that year, "At every reauthorization, we kept sweetening the deal for banks, sweetening the pot." He lamented the fact that this deal sweetening progressed until it reached the point where companies profited more from students defaulting than from students keeping their loans in good standing.

By 2006, student loans had fewer consumer protections than any other type of loan instrument in the nation's history. In 1976, Congress had passed a law making federally guaranteed student loans nondischargeable in bankruptcy; this meant that declaring bankruptcy did not erase the loan. Initially, a provision in the law stated that this only held true for five years, after which the loans could be discharged in bankruptcy. A further provision permitted the loans to be dischargeable if the debtor could prove undue hardship. In 1990, Congress extended the five years to seven, but watershed legislation that was part of the 1998 Higher Education Act reauthorization abolished this provision altogether. At that time, and still today, student loans are the only type of loan in U.S. history to be nondischargeable in bankruptcy. According to one borrower who found herself in bankruptcy court, "The judge told me not to come back unless I was in a wheelchair."

One might suspect that the student loan industry would be satisfied with the removal of this basic, standard consumer protection for federally guaranteed loans, but it still wasn't content. In 2005, the Bankruptcy Abuse Prevention and Consumer Protection Act was passed. Stealthily inserted into this bill was language that in effect made *all* student loans, even those that were *not* guaranteed by the federal government, nondischargeable in bankruptcy. This language was never debated by Congress, and the bill became law on October 17, 2005. The legislation was seen by experts as incontrovertible proof that the student loan industry, more than any other lending industry, held sway over the U.S. Congress.

In addition to removing bankruptcy protections, the amendments to the Higher Education Act eliminated all statutes of limitations for the collection of student loan debt. This opened up a whole new market: old loans from the 1970s and 1980s suddenly became collectible debt. Student loans were also specifically exempted from state usury laws, and they were even exempted from coverage under the Truth in Lending Act (TILA). In 1988, the Federal Trade Commission issued a determination that nonprofit, state-run student loan agencies did not have to adhere to the Fair Debt Collection and Practices Act. This meant that most student loan guarantors could ignore this legislation when pursuing defaulted borrowers.

From the beginning of the federally guaranteed student loan program, there were no obvious mechanisms for refinancing student loans after graduation and for consolidation of the loans. In other words, once a student graduated and consolidated his or her loans, he or she could never leave that lender, even if there were other lenders who were willing to offer better terms. The freedom to change lenders in order to find better terms for a loan is a consumer protection that is taken for granted in every other lending industry, but it is nonexistent for student loans. . . .

---

*It is imperative that standard consumer protections be returned to student loans.*

---

## Collection Powers

In addition to removing standard consumer protections, Congress passed legislation that made delinquent student loan debt highly lucrative for the student loan industry. This legislation allowed massive penalties and fees, and Congress permitted the industry to use draconian collection methods to recover this increased debt. Most of these congressional giveaways to the industry were included in the 1998 amendments to the Higher Education Act and were pushed fiercely by the student loan industry. "In American history, this is the most outrageous giveaway ever extended by the federal government to private lenders," says Barmak Nassirian, associate executive director of the American Association of Collegiate Registrars and Admissions Officers.

This legislation provided for collection rates of up to 25 percent to be applied to the debt. This meant that when borrowers defaulted on their loans, guarantors could take a quarter of every dollar the borrowers eventually repaid, money that would not be applied to the principal and interest on the debts, which the borrowers had been unable to afford to repay in the first place. This massive, unearned revenue stream going to the guarantors and to the collection agencies they contract with (agencies that are often owned by the original lenders) has not surprisingly led to usurious situations. . . .

## The Solution

The current student loan system in this country works extremely well for banks and quite well for the federal government, but it has effectively crippled millions of Americans. Ironically, their attempts to achieve the American dream through higher education have turned their lives into living nightmares from which they have no recourse. Surely, the present-day scenario is not what President [Lyndon] Johnson and the Congress of 1965 had in mind when they created the federal student loan system. Their intention was to assist Americans in bettering themselves, and thus the nation, through higher education; it was not to make them captive to an unethical financing system that penalizes the people who need aid most.

While experts on all sides of the student loan issue debate, conjecture, and argue about the best course forward for the student loan system, the most obvious solution is abundantly clear: it is imperative that standard consumer protections be returned to student loans.

# 4

# Student Loan Defaults Are the Result of Bad Decisions

*Jacob Sullum*

*Jacob Sullum is a senior editor at* Reason *and a nationally syndicated columnist.*

*Although Alan Collinge overstates the case against the student loan industry based on his own unfortunate experiences, he does make some valid points. Specifically, Collinge's recommendations that students be able to refinance the terms of their loans and discharge their debt in bankruptcy court merit consideration. However, Collinge is remiss in not stating that most people who have difficulty paying off their student loans have exercised poor judgment at some step along the way and thus bear some responsibility for their plight.*

My wife and I recently made the last payment on her federally backed Stafford loan from graduate school. She had borrowed $21,500, which is slightly more than the average for the two-thirds of four-year college students who take out loans and about half the average for graduate students who borrow. We made modest payments every month for about nine years, and now we're done. Given the extent to which my wife's degrees enhanced her earning ability, the loan was a sound investment.

## Most Students Do Not Default

My wife did not feel that her education had done her "far more harm than good," that it had condemned her to "a life-

Jacob Sullum, "A Lesson in Finance," *Wall Street Journal*, February 24, 2009. www.online .wsj.com. Copyright © 2009 by Creators Syndicate. Reproduced by permission.

time of indentured servitude" or that she was living in "student loan hell." Neither of us was driven to despair, divorce, suicide or expatriation by the constant pressure of crushing indebtedness and relentless collection agencies. In other words, our experience was very different from the horror stories that Alan Michael Collinge tells in "The Student Loan Scam" to reinforce his argument that student loans are "the most oppressive" type of debt "in our nation's history."

---

*The two-year default rate for federal student loans . . . is less than 5%.*

---

Student-loan data suggest that my wife's case is far more typical than the examples cited by Mr. Collinge, all of which involve people who defaulted on their loans and saw their debt mushroom as a result of penalties, collection fees and compound interest. According to the Education Department, the two-year default rate for federal student loans (both direct government loans and private loans backed by government guarantees and subsidies) is less than 5%. A separate Education Department analysis found that the 10-year default rate for college students who graduated in 1993 was less than 10%.

Mr. Collinge, who founded the political action committee StudentLoanJustice.org after the $38,000 he owed for his Caltech aerospace-engineering degrees nearly tripled in seven years because of default-related charges, tends to overgeneralize from his own "completely demoralizing" experience. Still, he highlights some genuinely troubling problems, including the government-fueled inflation in college costs (which continue rising partly because federal aid artificially boosts demand) and a lack of skepticism among borrowers about whether the costs are worth paying. He also describes the unfair treatment of borrowers who end up "ensnared in a web of debt" after making the wrong decision.

To help people out of that web, Mr. Collinge urges "standard consumer protections" for student borrowers. He makes a strong case for lifting restrictions on their ability to refinance their loans and for changing laws that prevent them from discharging their debt in bankruptcy court. He also rightly criticizes the insanely counterproductive policy of suspending people's professional licenses because they are struggling to pay off student loans.

In these and other respects, Mr. Collinge argues, major lenders—most conspicuously, the government-created company Sallie Mae—have rigged the rules against consumers and competitors. Sallie Mae, he writes, "lobbied its way to extreme profitability," using "an unfair advantage bestowed on it by Congress to take over the industry." Like Fannie Mae and Freddie Mac, Sallie Mae was created to expand credit by buying up loans. Its ties to the government were severed in 2004, and it is now the largest originator of student loans.

---

*The most common mistake of people who have trouble paying off student loans is failing to understand what they're getting into.*

---

## Defaulters Bear Responsibility

Still, Mr. Collinge underplays the extent to which defaulters bear responsibility for their plight. Although many are victims of circumstances beyond their control, almost all of the borrowers in the stories he tells showed bad judgment, inadequate effort or both. Elizabeth (who, like most of the debtors Mr. Collinge describes, is identified by first name only) borrowed $79,000 for an ultimately useless Bachelor of Fine Arts degree. Andrew borrowed $105,000 to study photography, then stopped "just short of receiving his bachelor's degree" because he decided the last year was "fluff." Mr. Collinge himself did academic research after school instead of seeking higher-paying industry work, then quit before he had a new job lined up.

But the most common mistake of people who have trouble paying off student loans is failing to understand what they're getting into, even overlooking details as basic as the interest rate and the consequences of missing a payment. Here Mr. Collinge does a real service with a chapter on what students need to consider when they make financial arrangements for school. He rightly warns them not simply to trust university financial-aid offices, which often have cozy relationships with specific lenders. He also urges students to investigate whether a particular degree from a particular institution is worth the cost. Such advice may seem like common sense, but Americans too often take for granted that college is a wise investment. As Elizabeth ruefully notes: "No one encourages you not to go to college."

## The Answer Is Not Consumer Protection

It's true that college graduates earn about $1 million more over their lifetimes than high-school graduates. But it's not clear how much of this difference can be attributed to higher education, since smarter people are more likely to finish college and have an employment advantage regardless of what they learn there. Furthermore, this number is an average, meaning that not everyone who goes to college benefits enough to justify the ever-rising cost.

Although Mr. Collinge calls the government-guaranteed student-loan system "obscenely inflationary," his solution—replacing loans with grants and direct subsidies to universities—does not address the imbalance between cost and benefit; it just shifts the cost around. If the problem is that the government has pushed excessive debt on people by mistakenly assuming that everyone should go to college—just as it pushed excessive debt on people by mistakenly assuming that everyone should own a home—it makes no sense to insulate consumers even further from the costs of their purchases. Better for students to pay their own way, borrowing if they must, from a private source, at the market rate. They might then think twice before getting in over their heads.

# 5

# The Recession Makes It Harder to Repay Student Loans

*Samantha Hillstrom*

*Samantha Hillstrom is a CNN production assistant and recent college graduate.*

*The burden of student loan debt is overwhelming for recent college graduates in entry-level positions. Monthly payments are too high and loan repayment terms are too short. The economic recession is exacerbating these woes, specifically in that lenders will not allow people to consolidate loans and stretch out repayment schedules. Student loans need reform, and debtors could benefit from the same kind of attention being paid to other types of debt during the recession.*

I'm about to talk about two little words that make most people cringe. The mere mention of these words usually incites the same reaction in everyone: a) fear b) denial c) a throbbing headache and d) the desire to run away screaming and crying and begging to go to a "happy place." Yes, I am talking about STUDENT LOANS. If you don't have one, you know someone who does and you sympathize with them. In the midst of the credit crisis, home foreclosures and bailout turmoil, the amount of debt that graduates are facing is overwhelming.

## Student Loans vs. Other Debt

I am 23-years-old, two years out of college and I am sitting on $115,000 of student debt. And based on my lender's loan terms, I only have roughly 12 years to pay it off. How much does that make my monthly payment, you ask? A whopping $1,200 a month. And let's just say my lifelong dream career in television doesn't lend itself to that. The only option my bank is giving me is to go on "graduated repayment plan." That means that for four years I will only be paying off the interest every month. How much is that? Well, $115,000 with interest rates between 4–8% ... that's about $600 a month and that doesn't even touch the principal amount. People don't pay off houses in 12 years and I am expected to pay off this student loan in an entry level position?

Some might say, "Sam, you shouldn't have gone to a private school in New York City if you wouldn't be able to pay it off." Well, I made a lot of mistakes when signing up for my loans, but I was uneducated on the process and on the repayment and now I'm stuck. I share the same anxiety as the families struggling to pay their mortgages. How was I ever to expect the financial crisis that was going to happen and where can I get some help?

*Why aren't student loans receiving the same attention, same care and forgiveness as every other loan in America?*

And why do I have such a short amount of time to pay off my loans? Because of the current financial crisis. Due to the economic downturn, my lender isn't consolidating loans. If I were able to consolidate, my repayment time would extend to 30 years ... just like a home mortgage. Now that wouldn't necessarily solve the problem, in that I would still owe more than $500 a month with the principal and interest, but it would buy me a bit more time and stretches out the money.

Here is my question: why aren't student loans receiving the same attention, same care and forgiveness as every other loan in America? I have to say that I am lucky to have a job right now and was especially lucky to get a job right out of college. Can you imagine what kind of pressure and stress the 2009 graduates are feeling in this time of uncertainty? Veterans of the workforce can't find work right now. What about the recent college grads with no work experience and tens of thousands of dollars of unforgivable debt underneath them?

There is a grain of hope that will come when the Income-Based Repayment Plan, part of the College Cost Reduction and Access Act of 2007, will take effect on July 1 [2009]. The program will cap off borrower's monthly payments at 10% of their gross income for 25 years with the rest of the debt being forgiven. However, that only applies to federal loans (which is only one of my four loans).

According to the Federal Education Department, in 2009, the amount of outstanding federal student loans is $544 billion, up $42 billion from last year. Where is our bailout? Where are our options? The default rate on student loans this year is already at 6.9%. That's a 13% increase from last year.

Recently, Rev. Jesse Jackson started a campaign called "Reduce the Rate" urging the [Barack] Obama administration to reduce the interest rates of student loans to 1% ... the same amount of interest the banks are getting.

Jackson's plan proposes the following ...

- Reduce the interest rate on all student loans to 1%.

- If banks can borrow at 1% or less, then so should our students.

- Extend the grace period before loan repayment begins from 6 months to 18 months for students who graduate.

- In these tough economic times, it takes a college graduate an average of 6 months to 1 year to find a job. The rules should reflect this reality.

- End the penalties assessed to schools for student loan defaults.

- Schools should not be held accountable for students who don't pay back their loans.

- Increase Pell Grants to cover the average yearly cost of a public 4 year institution instead of the amounts in the current stimulus package—$5,350 starting July 1 and $5,550 in 2010–2011

I chose to go to a private school and I chose to work in a field where the starting salaries are low. Does that mean that I chose to live a life of struggle, wondering how I am going to pay my rent, afford the basics of living and still stay in my chosen career field . . . all while putting up with high interest rates and an amount of debt that brings me to tears?

# 6

# Most People Easily Repay Their Student Loans

*James Monks*

*James Monks is an associate professor of economics at the Robins School of Business at the University of Richmond. He does research and consulting on the economics of higher education.*

*Most of what is currently being written about student loan debt grossly overstates the facts. Most students graduate with a manageable level of debt and the investment in education is more than made up for in higher-paying jobs.*

A great deal has been written about the onerous debt levels taken on by some of today's college students. Much of this discussion grossly overstates the true degree of burden that student loans place on most graduates. An overwhelming majority of students have reasonable and manageable levels of student loans. The typical four-year undergraduate student loan package totals approximately $19,000—no more than a midsized car. An automobile begins depreciating the minute you drive it off the lot, while one's college degree is an investment that will garner you a lifetime of higher earnings.

## Student Loans Are a Good Investment

From strictly an investment standpoint, a college education, even with $20,000 in student loans is a sound investment. The median earnings of a college graduate in the United States is approximately $50,000 per year, while the equivalent for a high school graduate is about $30,000 per year. So having to assume the usual package of student loans will pay for itself in just one year. Most students can easily repay their college loans and should not be deterred from borrowing sensibly.

Over the course of a 40-year career this difference in earnings translates into $800,000 (ignoring interest). Clearly, assuming a reasonable level of student loans is well worth the investment.

How difficult will it be to pay back one's student loans? A total of $20,000 in student loans would require a payment of approximately $250 per month for 10 years. Some personal financial planners suggest that student loans should not exceed 10 to 15 percent of one's gross earnings. Under this rule, an annual salary of between $20,000 to $30,000 would be sufficient to pay off the loan without due hardship. This level of income is below the earnings of most college graduates, and a new government program adjusts monthly payments based on one's level of income making repayment even more affordable. . . .

---

*With a dose of caution and planning students should not be deterred from taking out loans for their college education.*

---

Much has also been said about student loans forcing young people to make career choices that they otherwise would not have made (i.e. pushing them into more lucrative fields like business or law rather than careers in public service or the non-profit sector). But there's little convincing evidence that that is happening.

While some students may have onerously high levels of debt, most have quite manageable levels of borrowing. With a dose of caution and planning students should not be deterred from taking out loans for their college education.

# 7

# Student Loan Debt Should Be Forgiven to Stimulate the Economy

*Robert Applebaum*

*Robert Applebaum is an attorney and the founder and executive director of ForgiveStudentLoanDebt.com, as well as the creator of the Facebook group Cancel Student Loan Debt to Stimulate the Economy.*

*Forgiving student loan debt would provide a greater stimulus to the economy than any of the bailouts or stimulus packages that have been undertaken by the federal government. In return for receiving bailouts, banks should be required to forgive student loan debt. Such a measure would stimulate the economy because the money students would be spending to pay off their debt could go into consumer spending, which would fuel the economy and create jobs.*

President Obama [in February 2009] signed into law a $787 billion stimulus package on top of [President George W.] Bush's grossly mismanaged $700 billion TARP [Troubled Asset Relief Program] bailout from last September. Several weeks ago, the Federal Reserve basically printed an additional $1,000,000,000,000 to inject more funds into the monetary system which will undoubtedly have the effect of diminishing the purchasing power of the dollar. Since last fall the government has paid out *trillions* of dollars in bailouts, handouts, loans and giveaways, with no end in sight as our leaders try anything and everything to try and get our spiraling economy under control. While some of what Washington has already done may act to stimulate the economy, much of the trillions of dollars already spent will, no doubt, turn out to be just money wasted.

## Stimulus Not Working

Tax rebate checks *do not* stimulate the economy—history shows that people either spend such rebates on paying off credit card debt, or they simply save them, doing little to nothing to stimulate the economy. Presumably, that is why they were removed from the final version of the stimulus bill. The tax cuts that were included, however, amount to a whopping $44 per month for the rest of 2009, decreasing to an even more staggering $33 per month in 2010. This is hardly "relief" as it is likely to help nobody.

The Wall Street financial institutions, auto manufacturers, insurance companies and countless other irresponsible actors have now received TRILLIONS of taxpayer dollars (as demonstrated above, that's a number with 12 zeros at the end of it) to bail them out of their self-created mess. This, too, does nothing to stimulate the economy. It merely rewards bad behavior and does nothing to encourage institutional change. There is a better way.

How many times have we heard from our leaders in Washington that education is the key to solving all of our underlying societal problems? The so-called "Silver Bullet." For decades, presidents, senators and members of Congress have touted themselves as champions of education, yet they've done nothing to actually encourage the pursuit of one on an individual level.

Some of us have taken advantage of Federal Stafford Loans and other programs, including private loans, to finance higher education, presumably with the understanding that an advanced degree equates with higher earning power in the future. Many of us go into public service after attaining such degrees, something that's also repeatedly proclaimed as something society should encourage. Yet, the debt we've accrued to obtain such degrees have crippled our ability to reap the benefits of our educations, causing many to make the unfortunate choice of leaving public service so as to earn enough money to pay off that debt.

Our economy is in the tank. There isn't a reasonable economist alive who doesn't believe that the economy needs stimulating immediately. The only debate now centers on how to go about doing it. While the new stimulus plan contains some worthy provisions, very little of it will have a significant and immediate stimulating effect on the economy. The Obama Administration itself doesn't expect to see an upsurge in the economy until mid-to-late 2010.

---

*Forgiving student loan debt would have an* immediate *stimulating effect on the economy.*

---

## Forgive Student Loan Debt

Instead of funneling billions, if not *trillions* of additional dollars to banks, financial institutions, insurance companies and other institutions of greed that are responsible for the current economic crisis, why not allow educated, hardworking, middleclass Americans to get something in return? After all, they're our tax dollars too!

Forgiving student loan debt would have an *immediate* stimulating effect on the economy. Responsible people who did nothing other than pursue a higher education would have hundreds, if not thousands of extra dollars per month to spend, fueling the economy *now*. Those extra dollars being pumped into the economy would have a multiplying effect, unlike many of the provisions of the new stimulus package.

As a result, tax revenues would go up, the credit markets will unfreeze and jobs will be created. Consumer spending accounts for over two thirds of the entire U.S. economy and in recent months, consumer spending has declined at alarming, unprecedented rates. Therefore, it stands to reason that the fastest way to revive our ailing economy is to do something drastic to get consumers to spend.

This proposal would quickly revitalize the housing market, the ailing automobile industry, travel and tourism, durable goods and countless other sectors of the economy because the very people who sustain those sectors will automatically have hundreds or, in some cases, thousands of extra dollars per month to spend. The driving factor in today's economy is fear. Unless and until the middle class feels comfortable enough that they'll have their jobs, health insurance and extra money to spend not only next month, but the month after that, etc., the economy will not, indeed, cannot grow fast enough to stop the hemorrhaging.

---

*This is not about a free ride. This is about a new approach to economic stimulus.*

---

## Higher Education Loans Need Reform

Let me be clear. This is not about a free ride. This is about a new approach to economic stimulus, nothing more. To those who would argue that this proposal would cause the banking system to collapse or make student loans unavailable to future borrowers, please allow me to respond. I am in no way suggesting that the lending institutions who carry such debts on their balance sheets get legislatively shafted by having them wiped from their books. The banks and other financial institutions are going to get their money regardless because, in addition to the $700 [billion] TARP bailout, more bailout money is coming their way. This proposal merely suggests that in return for the trillions of dollars that has been and will continue to be handed over to the banks, educated, hardworking Americans who are saddled with student loan debt should get some relief as well, rather than sending those institutions another enormous blank check. Because the banks are being handed trillions of dollars anyway, there would be no danger of making funds unavailable to future borrowers.

To avoid the moral hazard that this plan could potentially create, going forward, the way higher education in this country is financed *MUST* be reformed. Requiring students to amass enormous debt just to receive an education is an untenable approach, as demonstrated by the ever-growing student loan default rates. Having a loan-based system rather than one based on grants and scholarships or, ideally, public funding, has, over time, begun to have the unintended consequence of discouraging people from seeking higher education at all. That is no way for America to reclaim the mantle of the land of opportunity.

---

*A well-educated workforce benefits society as a whole.*

---

A well-educated workforce benefits society as a whole, not just the students who receive a higher education. It is often said that an undergraduate degree today is the equivalent of a high school [HS] diploma 30 or 40 years ago. Accepting the premise as true that society does, in fact, place the same value on an undergraduate degree today as it did on a HS diploma 30 or 40 years ago, then what is the rationale for cutting off public funding of education after the 12th grade? It seems to me that there is some dissonance in our values that needs to be reconciled. That, however, cannot come to pass until the millions of us already shackled with student loan debt are freed from the enormous economic burdens we're presently carrying.

## Helping Students and Helping the Economy

Many of the vocal nay-sayers to this proposal seem intent on ignoring the fact that Washington IS going to spend *trillions* of dollars, likely in the form of handing blank checks over to more and more banks, as a way of getting the economy under control. Normative assessments of how things should be are fine, but they don't reflect reality. Accepting the premise that Washington *will* spend trillions of dollars in unprecedented ways (a good portion of which will just be trial and error, since we're in uncharted waters), what is the argument against directly helping middle class people who are struggling, rather than focusing solely on the banks and other financial institutions responsible for crisis to begin with?

Further accepting that there is an aggregate amount of outstanding student loan debt totaling approximately $550 Billion, (that's Billion with a B, not a T), one is forced to ask again, what is the objection to helping real people with real hardships when all we're talking about is a relative drop in the bucket as compared with what will be spent to dig us out of this hole?

In a perfect world, I share these biases towards personal responsibility and having people pay back what they owe and making good on the commitments they've made. But we don't live in a perfect world and the global economy, not just the U.S. economy, is in a downward spiral, the likes of which *nobody* truly knows how to fix.

This proposal will immediately free up money for hardworking, educated Americans, giving them more money in their pockets *every month*, addressing the very real psychological aspects of the recession as much as the financial ones. Is it the only answer? No, of course not. But could it help millions of hardworking people who struggle every month to get by? Absolutely. Given the current economic climate, as well as the plans to spend trillions of additional dollars that are in the works, one must wonder what is so objectionable about giving a real helping hand to real people with real struggles.

[It's] 2009 and the new Obama Administration is supposed to be about change. Nothing in the new economic stimulus package represents a significant departure from the way Washington has always operated—it's merely a different set of priorities on a higher scale, but it's certainly not materially different from any other economic stimulus package passed during the past few decades. Washington cannot simply print and borrow money to get us out of this crisis. We The People, however, can get this economy moving NOW. All we need is relief from debt that was accrued under the now-false promise that higher education equates with higher earnings.

Free us of our obligations to repay our out-of-control student loan debt and *we*, the hardworking, middle-class Americans who drive this economy will spend those extra dollars *now*.

# 8

# Forgiving Student Loan Debt Would Be Irresponsible

*Brian Kumnick*

*Brian Kumnick is a content optimization analyst at FindLaw, a legal information website.*

*Increasing attention is being paid to the problem of student loan debt, and there are some reasonable as well as unreasonable solutions. The approach outlined by Robert Applebaum, which is to simply forgive student loan debt, would be irresponsible. However, there are other suggestions worth pursuing, such as Senator Dick Durbin's recommendation that bankruptcy rules should be amended to allow student loans to be discharged.*

Everyone wants a bailout these days. Everywhere you look you'll see a group that thinks the U.S. Treasury should issue them a blank check or two to ease their financial pain. Graduates of this country's institutions of higher learning are no different.

## An Irresponsible Plan

We will avoid throwing around a lot of numbers here as we summarize. College and graduate school are expensive. Students borrow an awful lot of money to earn degrees which, their schools promise them, will provide an ample return on investment. But graduates often find themselves earning far less than they expected, or even unable to find work in the field they've trained for. Result: monthly loan payments that eat up a huge chunk of income, stretched out over 10- and 20-year repayment schedules. Many borrowers end up right where they were before they entered school: living in financial uncertainty or barely getting by.

Making matters worse is that federal law makes student loans exceptionally difficult to include in a bankruptcy. Both federal and private loans are now excepted from bankruptcy discharge, unless the debtor petitions for a determination of "undue hardship."

Is there anything that can help? A recent *USA Today* article highlighted a couple of approaches being suggested to help address what may or may not be a student loan repayment crisis.

Robert Applebaum, a lawyer (of course), is emerging as a spokesman for the full-blown debt-forgiveness option. His proposal is as follows: Congress should pass legislation forgiving student loan debt. Yes, that's the plan in all its detail, unless we are missing something on this proposal page. Unburdening debtors via a forgiveness plan will stimulate our battered economy with a massive increase in consumer spending, the argument goes. Everyone wins. No word on how (or if) all those lenders would get compensated, but the lack of detail in Applebaum's plan has not made it unpopular: Applebaum's Facebook group (of course) has a membership in the hundreds of thousands.

---

*The Applebaum debt-forgiveness proposal is over-the-top, dangerous, and fraught with moral hazard.*

---

## A More Moderate Approach

*USA Today* also notes that Senator Dick Durbin (D-Ill.) is taking a more cautious and probably more viable approach, seeking to reform the bankruptcy rules to allow private student loans to be dischargeable. Lenders have always argued that making it easier to include student loans in bankruptcy will ultimately drive loan costs higher, but of course one could say that about any kind of debt, and yet many debts are in fact still dischargeable. This plan may strike the right balance and offer some hope for the many who are already on the edge of bankruptcy.

Finally, according to the *Guardian*, in the UK, student-loan interest rates are being adjusted downward to 0%. Here is a much less drastic version of the Applebaum plan, something that might offer relief to all borrowers (and presumably stimulate consumer spending) without unduly harming lenders. Perhaps interest-free loans would be too much to ask for, but a significant rate cut may be in order.

It should be obvious where we stand here. The Applebaum debt-forgiveness proposal is over-the-top, dangerous, and fraught with moral hazard. Other plans are more moderate, socially responsible, and potentially viable. But sign us up with Applebaum. We've got loans too, after all, and there's a reason we call ourselves *Greedy* Associates.

# 9

# Pell Grants Are Needed to Make America Competitive

*Pat Garofalo*

*Pat Garofalo is a senior economics researcher at the Center for American Progress and a blogger at the Center for American Progress Action Fund.*

*The key to America's future is a well-educated workforce. Legislators looking at deficit reduction are short-sighted if they recommend cuts to Pell Grants, a program that helps America remain economically competitive.*

One of the least publicized achievements of the 111th Congress is the Student Aid and Fiscal Responsibility Act, which passed as part of the health care reform package that was signed into law by President Barack Obama in March. SAFRA cut billions of dollars in senseless subsidies that private companies were receiving to originate federal student loans in favor of originating all federal student loans directly through the Department of Education. The money saved is being used to expand the Pell Grant program, which provides low-income students with grants to finance their higher education.

SAFRA is a key piece of legislation that will pump $100 billion into the economy via the increased earnings of students who will have new access to Pell Grants, according to an analysis by the Center for American Progress Action Fund.

But the Pell program is already facing a new challenge—a shortfall in funding due to a combination of the economic stimulus package ending and increased demand. And with the incoming class of conservative lawmakers looking to slash the federal budget, access to higher education for millions of American students is at stake.

For the 2011 fiscal year, the Pell Grant program is facing a roughly $5.7 billion shortfall at a time when demand for grants is increasing due to the lingering effects of the Great Recession. If the shortfall isn't closed, the maximum grant under the program will be cut by about $845 for the 2011 academic year. In all, about 9 million students will have their awards reduced if additional funding is not approved.

---

*Reducing the supply of Pell Grants . . . would be sacrificing America's long-term economic strength on the altar of short-term deficit reduction.*

---

The trouble is that conservatives on Capitol Hill are draping themselves in supposed fiscal responsibility and may refuse to cover the shortfall. In their much-ballyhooed "Pledge to America," for instance, House Republicans promised to reduce nondefense discretionary spending back to the 2008 level, which would cut about $9 billion from the Pell Grant program. The incoming chairmen of the House Budget and Education committees, Reps. Paul Ryan (R-WI) and John Kline (R-MN), respectively, are reportedly eyeing Pell reductions already. "If John Kline doesn't fire the first volley, Paul Ryan in the budget committee is going to," a Republican staffer told *Inside Higher Ed.*

Cutting Pell Grants, particularly amid a weak economic recovery, would be extremely foolhardy. For one thing, according to the National Center for Education Statistics, Pell recipients largely come from traditionally underserved communities. They are "more likely to be female and first-generation college students, and less likely to be white than those who don't receive the grants."

But keeping the Pell Grant program fully funded is about more than ensuring adequate access to higher education for these disadvantaged students (though that, by itself, is a worthy goal). It's also about the country's economic competitiveness, which depends on having a highly educated, 21st century workforce. And at the moment, America has a falling level of educational attainment after leading the world for most of the postwar period.

According to the College Board, America is now 12th worldwide in percentage of 25-to-34-year-olds with a college degree, trailing, among others, Russia, New Zealand, South Korea, Ireland, and Israel. Just 35 percent of 18-to-24-year-olds were enrolled in some form of higher education in 2008, according to the National Center on Public Policy and Education, compared to more than 50 percent of South Koreans.

Canada is currently number one in terms of educational attainment. To retake that top spot, the United States would have to add 1 million college degrees per year through 2025, in addition to the 2 million annual degrees that are in the pipeline already. By 2025, according to estimates by the Lumina Foundation, our nation will be short 16 million college-educated workers. This will have real consequences for both the economy as a whole and for individual workers.

"Since 1975, the average earnings of high school dropouts and high school graduates fell in real terms (by 15 percent and 1 percent, respectively) while those of college graduates rose by 19 percent," the Lumina Foundation found. "In other words, the economic benefits of higher education—both for individuals and society—are growing." Today, the average annual income of a college-educated person is $43,000 while someone with just a high school diploma averages $27,000.

America's supply of human capital and its ability to remain economically competitive with the rest of the world hinges on its ability to develop a highly educated workforce. The Student Aid and Fiscal Responsibility Act was an important step in the right direction. Reducing the supply of Pell Grants would have the opposite effect and would be sacrificing America's long-term economic strength on the altar of short-term deficit reduction. That is not a trade any policymaker should be willing to make.

# 10

# Pell Grants Raise the Cost of College and Cause Education Inequality

*Richard Vedder*

*Richard Vedder is a professor of economics at Ohio University and an adjunct scholar at the American Enterprise Institute.*

*Despite arguments to the contrary, there is no proof that Pell Grants have played a role in promoting access to a college degree in America. On the contrary, Pell Grants have had the opposite effect, decreasing the demand for higher education because they have raised the cost of obtaining a college degree.*

I have three points I wish to make. . . .

First, the law of unintended consequences has led to higher education outcomes far different than intended as federal student assistance has expanded over the past 35 years. For example, I think it is hard to demonstrate that enhanced federal assistance has either significantly expanded college participation or brought about much greater access to higher education by those who are financially disadvantaged. In their totality, federal programs have contributed to the "tuition bubble" that has been an unfortunate feature of American higher education. The proposed additional expansions contemplated will

Richard Vedder, "Statement of Richard Vedder, Director, Center of College Affordability and Productivity, Distinguished Professor of Economics, Ohio University, Adjunct Scholar, American Enterprise Institute, to the Committee on Education and Labor," centerforcollegeaffordability.org, May 21, 2009. Copyright © 2009 by Center for College Affordability and Productivity (CCAP). Reproduced by permission.

likely not have the intended effects on student participation, access and equality of educational opportunity.

Second, the proposal to end the Federal Family Education Loan (FFEL) program and replace it with direct federal student lending will have negative consequences on students quite independent of the alleged financial consequences to the federal government. People like to have choices, and private loan providers do not follow the one-size-fits-all model implicit in the federal direct loan program. I understand that there is some dispute on the potential savings arising from a budgetary perspective to going to direct loans, and I suspect the true savings are in fact exaggerated, but even if that is not the case, the move away from diversity in provider offerings is a step backward.

Third, the proposal to sharply expand the Pell Grant program by making it an entitlement offered to far more students than presently, with larger sized grants, is fiscally irresponsible. It may even be a potential factor in raising college costs, statutory provisions to control costs notwithstanding.

## Grants Do Not Increase Enrollment

Turning to the first point, in their latest book Harvard professors Claudia Goldin and Lawrence Katz argue that the rate of increase in educational attainment in the United States slowed significantly beginning in the mid 1970s. Speaking of the twentieth century, Goldin and Katz assert that "during the first three quarters of the century educational attainment rose rapidly, but during the last quarter of the century, it stagnated." It is not entirely a coincidence, I think, that the major federal grant program, Pell Grants, and, even more importantly, federal student loans, began around 1975.

From the mid 1950s to the mid 1970s, higher education enrollments almost quadrupled, before Pell Grants existed and before federal student loans were large and universally available. Tuition tax credits were decades away during this era of huge enrollment growth. The era of exploding federal financial assistance has paralleled a significant slowdown in enrollment growth. From 1955 to 1975, enrollments grew at a compounded annual rate approaching 7.5 percent a year. From 1975 to 2007, enrollments rose under 1.6 percent a year, not dramatically more than population growth. In the one-third of a century since 1975, when Pell Grants were just getting underway, enrollment growth has far less than doubled, at a time that the American population has grown well over 40 percent. America has fallen behind a double digit number of nations in the proportion of young adults with bachelor's degrees. The notion that federal financial aid has promoted college access in the United States is more a myth than a factual reality. Large expansion of these programs will almost certainly not promote higher access; this is particularly true of the student loan programs, which are quantitatively larger in importance than Pell Grants, which have some possibility to have positive access attributes.

---

*Student aid potentially has increased the demand for higher education far more than it has increased supply, raising the price of colleges to students.*

---

Now I am aware that other things are occurring in this era as well. Changes in income, the cost of college, the college–high school earnings differential, and changing state appropriations for colleges are a few variables that are relevant. Many of them, however, changed in ways that should increase enrollment. The point I am trying to make here is not that rising federal aid reduced the growth in participation itself, but rather that it is not correct to say that federal loan and grant programs have dramatically improved educational attainment in the U.S.—if anything, the evidence suggests the impact of the programs likely has been to lower, not raise participation.

# Federal Aid Increases the Cost of College

Why might that be? Most importantly, student aid potentially has increased the demand for higher education far more than it has increased supply, raising the price of colleges to students. If the price increases are substantial—as indeed they have been—it is possible that the enrollment reducing effects of higher federal student financial aid has more than offset the enrollment enhancement effects arising from lowering net effective prices to the student arising from student aid. If sticker prices have risen more than tuition discounting, counting federal aid as a form of that discounting, it is easy to arrive at a solution where the total college participation effect of student aid is negative. To be sure, this is a simple generalization, and Pell Grants have probably had significantly different effects than student loans and tuition tax credits, but in aggregate the federal programs have almost certainly pushed the cost of higher education upwards.

Moreover, the era of greater federal aid is a period of declining equality of educational opportunity. When Chairman [George] Miller completed his higher education, 1972, before a single Pell Grant had been awarded, persons from the top quartile of the income distribution had about six times as likely a probability of earning a bachelor's degree by age 24 as persons in the bottom quartile. Today, the upper income student has nearly eight times the probability of getting a degree. . . . Although there has been modest improvement in recent years, inequality is greater today than it was when the Pell Grant program began in the mid-1970s.

Part of the explanation for this trend relates to non-aid related factors, such as the fact that some schools have deliberately restricted supply, especially for marginally achieving students, many of whom are low income, as part of an academic arms race where colleges try to gain prestige in published rankings that depend in part on the quality of students admitted and the proportion of students denied admission. But part no doubt relates to the fact that student loan programs have become very much a phenomenon utilized by comparatively affluent students who come from families with incomes exceeding the national median.

Department of Education data affirm this. For example, take Stafford loans. For dependent students from families of less than $20,000 income, 47.2 percent received Stafford loans in 2007–08, about the same percent (45.1 percent) as for students from families with over $80,000 income, a figure well above the median family income. Over 35 percent of students from families with over $100,000 income received such loans.

The President has spoken about his goal of dramatically expanding college participation. This is not the forum to discuss whether that goal is either practically reasonable or desirable. However, I can say that I very much doubt that the totality of the proposed legislative changes with respect to student aid will substantially further either the president's goal with respect to participation or with respect to equalizing educational opportunities among Americans.

## Students Deserve Choices

Regarding the second point, it may be true that the direct student loan program will reduce the budgeted outlays of the federal government, but even the extent to which that is true I believe is open to debate. For example, with expanded lending occurring in a deep recession environment, can one predict with any accuracy student loan default rates? As the ratio of debts to starting postgraduate incomes rise, will not default on loans become a bigger issue? Indeed, are we perhaps setting some students up to fail, luring marginally qualified students to college, only to have them not succeed in graduating, but nonetheless incurring large debts?

But I want to emphasize a different point. Our government is one of the people, by the people, and for the people. And the people prefer choices to monopoly. We rejoice that technology has robbed the Post Office of much of its monopoly power, and reduced our reliance on unreliable delivery and long lines to buy stamps. Similarly, we find it far more pleasant to buy insurance for a new car from competitive insurance agents and companies than buying license plates for the car from the monopolistic Bureau of Motor Vehicles. Colleges have rightly mostly shunned the direct lending program because of the additional choices and services offered by private providers. To win business, the private providers have to please the customer, an incentive totally lacking if the government is the only major game in town. Are private providers earning monopoly profits from federal subsidies? Hardly, if recent exits from the industry and the stock prices of loan providers are valid indicators of profitability, as I think they are. I would note that in the past year [May 2008–2009], the price of Sallie Mae stock has plunged 71 percent, the Student Loan Corporation stock has fallen 62 percent, and that of Nelnet by 38 percent. The loss in wealth to stockholders, including pension funds, in these companies, in addition to the potential unemployment of workers, is another reason you should give pause before endorsing the [Barack] Obama Administration proposals, the testimony of Sallie Mae notwithstanding. Have some private providers engaged in dubious ethical or outright illegal practices in consort with universities? Probably, and they should be punished severely, perhaps by being forced to attend and write summaries of 100 congressional hearings, or some other form of near torture. But we should not deny students the opportunity to choose amongst multiple options because of a few ethically challenged individuals or institutions.

Moreover, any federal financing of student loans requires additional borrowing from a government that has engaged in extraordinarily reckless long term expansions in its own debt, an expansion that foists a large burden on future generations of Americans. The Congressional Budget Office tells us we will have nine trillion dollars in deficits over the next decade, which on average is more than $100,000 debt for each family of four. To me, this is not only fiscally irresponsible, but downright immoral, since powerful persons, namely Congress and the Administration, are foisting burdens on young persons who adults should be protecting rather than harming—all in the name of short term political expediency. I am a patriotic American who loves our representative democracy, but with a heavy heart I must say, "shame on you."

Moreover, the present value of the unfunded liabilities of federal entitlement programs now well exceeds 50 trillion dollars, or the entire value of the physical capital stock of this nation. Most of this is the Medicare and Social Security entitlement programs. It is the height of irresponsibility to add to that liability; rather, you should be working to whittle it down, for example, by reforming Social Security.

## Aid Leads to Educational Inequality

Let me also reiterate that the empirical evidence is unclear in my judgment whether the Pell Grant program is an effective means of promoting equal educational opportunity. My colleague Andrew Gillen has shown beautifully how Pell Grants can have positive enrollment effects without severe effects on tuition costs, but there is some empirical evidence to the contrary, and the historical evidence does not make one confident that Pell Grants have powerfully promoted equal economic opportunity given rising higher education inequality. Proposed revisions in the Perkins loan program are harder to interpret owing to a lack of detailed explanations, but both my colleague Dr. Gillen and I suspect that the proposals will serve to raise tuition costs.

Also, a significant expansion in federal aid programs, especially student loans, almost certainly will contribute to the tuition price explosion. When someone else is paying the bills, costs always rise, and all sorts of clever regulatory moves to stop this will simply either lead to denied student access, reductions in academic quality, and/or increased university bureaucracies, already obscenely large. In the past, the Pell Grant program has had relatively little tuition fee impact in my judgment, for reasons explained in the enclosed study by Dr. Gillen. But as Pell Grants increasingly become a middle class entitlement going to students who otherwise would go to college anyway, and grow in size, the probability that Pell expansion will be relatively tuition fee neutral becomes more problematic. Pell Grants are dwarfed in magnitude by student loan programs in any case. In total, the law of unintended consequences is at work, as the tuition bubble that federal policies such as student loans and tax credits have contributed to have undone any positive impacts that otherwise would occur.

# 11

# For-Profit Education Resembles the Subprime Mortgage Industry

*Steven Eisman*

*Steven Eisman is portfolio manager of the FrontPoint Financial Services Fund.*

*The student loan industry shows significant parallels with the subprime mortgage industry, whose tactics decimated the economy. In the subprime mortgage industry, the loan originators reaped all the rewards regardless of whether the loan borrowers ultimately defaulted. The student loan industry is similarly structured, so that the for-profit colleges get paid whether or not the loan defaults. Poorly aligned incentives are at the root of the problem in both industries. To fix the excessive default rate on loans at for-profit schools, the for-profit education industry must be made to bear some of the costs for defaulted loans.*

My name is Steven Eisman and I am the portfolio manager of the FrontPoint Financial Services Fund. My firm has spent a great deal of time studying the For-Profit education industry and understanding how it operates and derives its revenue. It has been an eye opening experience. Until recently, I thought that there would never again be an opportunity to be involved with an industry as socially destructive as the subprime mortgage industry. I was wrong. The For-Profit Education Industry has proven equal to the task.

Steven Eisman, "Subprime Goes to College," Testimony Before the US Senate Committee on Health, Education, Labor, and Pensions, June 24, 2010. www.help.senate.gov. Copyright © 2010 by US Senate: Committee on Health, Education, Labor, and Pensions. Reproduced by permission.

## The Industry Reaps All the Rewards

My testimony today comes largely from a recent presentation I gave at an investor conference entitled "Subprime goes to College." The for-profit industry has grown at an extreme and unusual rate, driven by easy access to government sponsored debt in the form of Title IV student loans [Title IV of the Higher Education Act of 1965 provides for financial aid for students], where the credit is guaranteed by the government. Thus, the government, the students and the taxpayer bear all the risk and the for-profit industry reaps all the rewards. This is similar to the subprime mortgage sector in that the subprime originators bore far less risk than the investors in their mortgage paper.

The for-profit education industry accounts for 9% of the students, 25% of all Title IV disbursements but 44% of all defaults. And the President of the largest for-profit institution is paid nearly 25x the compensation level of the President of Harvard. There is something wrong with this statistical progression.

---

*The government, the students and the taxpayer bear all the risks and the for-profit industry reaps all the rewards.*

---

In the past 10 years, the for-profit education industry has grown 5–10 times the historical rate of traditional post secondary education. From 1987 through 2000, the amount of total Title IV dollars received by students of for-profit schools fluctuated between $2 and $4 billion per annum. But when the [George W.] Bush administration took over the reins of government, the DOE [Department of Education] gutted many of the rules that governed the conduct of this industry. Once the floodgates were opened, the industry embarked on 10 years of unrestricted massive growth.

Federal dollars flowing to the industry exploded to over $21 billion, a 450% increase.

At many major for-profit institutions, federal Title IV loan and grant dollars now comprise close to 90% of total revenues, up significantly vs. 2001. And this growth has driven even more spectacular company profitability and wealth creation for industry executives. For example, ITT Educational Services (ESI), one of the larger companies in the industry, has a roughly 40% operating margin vs. the 7%–12% margins of other companies that receive major government contracts. ESI is more profitable on a margin basis than even Apple.

This growth is purely a function of government largesse, as Title IV has accounted for more than 100% of revenue growth. Here is one of the more upsetting statistics. In fiscal 2009, Apollo, the largest company in the industry, grew total revenues by $833 million. Of that amount, $1.1 billion came from Title IV federally-funded student loans and grants. More than 100% of the revenue growth came from the federal government. But of this incremental $1.1 billion in federal loan and grant dollars, the company spent only an incremental $99 million on faculty compensation and instructional costs— that's 9 cents on every dollar received from the government going towards actual education. The rest went to marketing and paying the executives.

---

*The for-profit model seeks to recruit those with the greatest financial need and put them in high cost institutions.*

---

## For-Profits Market to the Poor

One major reason why the industry has taken an ever increasing share of government dollars is that it has turned the typical education model on its head. And here is where the subprime analogy becomes very clear.

There is a traditional relationship between matching means and cost in education. Typically, families of lesser financial means seek lower cost institutions in order to maximize the available Title IV loans and grants—thereby getting the most out of every dollar and minimizing debt burdens. Families with greater financial resources often seek higher cost institutions because they can afford it more easily.

The for-profit model seeks to recruit those with the greatest financial need and put them in high cost institutions. This formula maximizes the amount of Title IV loans and grants that these students receive.

With billboards lining the poorest neighborhoods in America and recruiters trolling casinos and homeless shelters (and I mean that literally), the for-profits have become increasingly adept at pitching the dream of a better life and higher earnings to the most vulnerable of society.

## Promised Education Not Delivered

But if the industry in fact educated its students and got them good jobs that enabled them to receive higher incomes and to pay off their student loans, everything I've just said would be irrelevant.

So the key question to ask is—what do these students get for their education? In many cases, NOT much, not much at all.

Here is an example of an education promised and never delivered. . . . [I refer to] an article detailing a Corinthian Colleges–owned Everest College campus in California whose students paid $16,000 for an 8-month course in medical assisting. Upon nearing completion, the students learned that not only would their credits not transfer to any community or four-year college, but also that their degree is not recognized by the American Association for Medical Assistants. Hospitals refuse to even interview graduates.

## High Drop Out and Default Rates

But let's leave aside the anecdotal evidence of this poor quality of education. After all the industry constantly argues that there will always be a few bad apples. So let's put aside the anecdotes and just look at the statistics. If the industry provided the right services, drop out rates and default rates should be low.

Let's first look at drop out rates. Companies don't fully disclose graduation rates, but using both DOE data, company-provided information and admittedly some of our own assumptions regarding the level of transfer students, we calculate [that] drop out rates at most for-profit schools are 50%+ per year.

How good could the product be if drop out rates are so stratospheric? These statistics are quite alarming, especially given the enormous amount of debt most for-profit students must borrow to attend school.

We have every expectation that the industry's default rates are about to explode. Because of the growth in the industry and the increasing search for more students, we are now back to late 1980s levels of lending to for-profit [college-enrolled] students on a per student basis. Back then defaults were off the charts and fraud was commonplace.

Default rates are already starting to skyrocket. It's just like subprime—which grew at any cost and kept weakening its underwriting standards to grow.

By the way, the default rates the industry reports are artificially low. There are ways the industry can and does manipulate the data to make their default rates look better.

But don't take my word for it. The industry is quite clear what it thinks the default rates truly are. ESI and COCO [Corinthian Colleges] supplement Title IV loans with their own private loans. And they provision 50%–60% up front for those loans. Believe me, when a student defaults on his or her private loans, they are defaulting on their Title IV loans too.

There is no such thing as a profitable loan where the loan loss provision is 50%–60%. So why do these companies make unprofitable non-FFELP [Federal Family Education Loan Program] loans? The private loan is much smaller than the FFELP loan and the companies don't bear any losses on FFELP loans, only on private loans. As a result, the losses on the private loans are just loss leaders to get more students in the door.

## Manipulated Statistics

Let me just pause here for a second to discuss manipulation of statistics. There are two key statistics. No school can get more than 90% of its revenue from the government and 2 year cohort default rates cannot exceed 25% for 3 consecutive years. Failure to comply with either of these rules and you lose Title IV eligibility. Lose Title IV eligibility and you're company's a zero.

With respect to the default statistics, it is my belief that they are manipulated. Since the rule currently revolves around the 2 year default rate, the companies have every incentive to keep that statistic below 25%.

Isn't it amazing that Apollo's percentage of revenue from Title IV is 89% and not over 90%? How lucky can they be? We believe (and many recent lawsuits support) that schools actively manipulate the receipt, disbursement and especially the return of Title IV dollars to their students to remain under the 90/10 threshold. And again, unprofitable private student loans is also a way to keep below the 90/10 threshold.

---

*In a sense, these companies are marketing machines masquerading as universities.*

---

The bottom line is that as long as the government continues to flood the for-profit education industry with loan dollars AND the risk for these loans is borne solely by the students and the government, THEN the industry has every incentive to grow at all costs, compensate employees based on enrollment, influence key regulatory bodies and manipulate reported statistics—ALL TO MAINTAIN ACCESS TO THE GOVERNMENT'S MONEY.

In a sense, these companies are marketing machines masquerading as universities. And when the Bush administration eliminated almost all the restrictions on how the industry is allowed to market, the machine went into overdrive.

## For-Profits Control Accreditation

How do such schools stay in business? The answer is to control the accreditation process. The scandal here is exactly akin to the rating agency role in subprime securitizations.

There are two kinds of accreditation—national and regional. Accreditation bodies are non-governmental, non-profit peer-reviewing groups. Schools must earn and maintain proper accreditation to remain eligible for Title IV programs. The relationship of the for-profit education industry and the national accrediting boards is, in my view, similar to the relationship between the rating agencies and investment banks. There, Wall Street paid the rating agencies handsomely for ratings on subprime securitizations that turned out to be overly optimistic. Here, the industry, we believe, controls the national accrediting bodies by actually sitting on the boards of those very same institutions. The lunatics are running the asylum.

Historically, most for-profit schools are nationally accredited but national accreditation holds less value than regional accreditation. The latest trend of for-profit institutions is to acquire the dearly coveted Regional Accreditation through the outright purchase of small, financially distressed non-profit institutions and then put that school on-line. In March 2005, BPI acquired the regionally accredited Franciscan University of the Prairies and renamed it Ashford University. On the date of purchase, Franciscan (now Ashford) had 312 students. BPI took that school online and at the end of 2009 it had 54,000 students.

When I was researching the subprime mortgage industry in 2005 and 2006, I found that not every lender was bad—just most of them. A few subprime lenders actually used considerable discretion and really tried to make good loans to lower-income borrowers that made sense for them. In the for-profit industry, the same is probably true. There are probably a few good institutions that truly try to educate their students.

---

*The best way to change this industry's conduct is to change the law and force it to bear some of the losses that it creates.*

---

## Incentives Are at the Root of the Problem

The core of the problem in both the subprime and the for-profit education industries is a problem of incentives. In subprime, brokers were incentivized to make as many loans as possible because they were paid on volume. They faced no risk of loss due to bad decision-making because the loans were sold off to investors. In for-profit education, every segment of the institution is incentivized to enroll as many students as possible—recruiters are paid on volume, instructors are compensated based on completions, and executives and shareholders are paid based on growth. None bear the risk of loss should the students not get their money's worth or even worse, default on their loans. The incentives to grow far outweigh the incentives to educate. And thus, like in subprime lending, rather than having a fundamentally sound industry with a few bad actors, you have a fundamentally unsound industry with few good ones.

Therefore, the best way to change this industry's conduct is to change the law and force it to bear some of the losses that it creates. . . .

Let me end by driving the subprime analogy to its ultimate conclusion. By late 2004, it was clear to me and my partners that the mortgage industry had lost its mind and a society-wide calamity was going to occur. It was like watching a train wreck with no ability to stop it. Who could you complain to?—The rating agencies?—they were part of the machine. Alan Greenspan?—he was busy making speeches that every American should take out an ARM mortgage loan. The OCC [Office of the Comptroller of the Currency]?—its chairman, John Dugan, was busy suing state attorney generals, preventing them from even investigating the subprime mortgage industry.

Are we going to do this all over again? We just loaded up one generation of Americans with mortgage debt they can't afford to pay back. Are we going to load up a new generation with student loan debt they can never afford to pay back? The industry is now 25% of Title IV money on its way to 40%. If its growth is stopped now and it is policed, the problem can be stopped. It is my hope that this Administration sees the nature of the problem and begins to act now.

But if nothing is done, then we are on the cusp of a new social disaster. If present trends continue, over the next ten years almost $500 billion of Title IV loans will have been funneled to this industry. We estimate total defaults of $275 billion, and because of fees associated with defaults, for-profit students will owe $330 billion on defaulted loans over the next 10 years.

# 12

# For-Profit Education Does Not Resemble the Subprime Mortgage Industry

*Harris N. Miller*

*Harris N. Miller is president and CEO of the Career College Association.*

*Steven Eisman's comparison of the for-profit college market to the subprime mortgage industry is wrongheaded, simplistic, and self-serving. Unlike in the subprime mortgage industry, there is no bubble artificially driving demand. The need for higher education is real and will not go away. Additionally, if too many of its students drop out, a school no longer has access to Title IV (of the Higher Education Act of 1965) student aid. Eisman is a short seller, meaning that he makes money when stocks drop, and thus he has a financial interest in attacking the for-profit education industry.*

In a recent speech in New York and in testimony submitted for tomorrow's Senate HELP [Health, Education, Labor & Pensions] Committee hearing, Steven Eisman, a portfolio manager at FrontPoint Financial Services Fund, castigated the private sector higher education community, making an absurd comparison to the subprime mortgage industry. Mr. Eisman is a noted short seller, accorded recognition for his role in predicting the collapse of the subprime mortgage lending marketplace. A short seller is someone who makes money when stock prices of publicly traded companies drop, often precipitously.

## There Is No Higher Education Bubble

Given their role in predicting such declines, short sellers are modern Cassandras [an ancient Greek prophetess doomed to announce coming disasters], constantly warning of economic doom and gloom. Just like stopped clocks, once in a while they are right. To the extent that through careful review and analysis of facts they draw attention to fraud, abuse or other miscarriages of investor trust, they perform a useful watchdog service.

When they cross the line, however, and exaggerate, exploit or even invent information to raise doubts, short sellers are an impediment to properly functioning markets and harmful to shareholders and stakeholders alike. When among the stakeholders are a population of working adult and lower income students, many pursuing higher education for the first time in order to achieve better lives for themselves and their families and benefitting our country's economy, particular care should be given to the line between vigilance and vitriol. For whatever reason, Mr. Eisman not only crossed it, he ignored it altogether.

How so? Comparing the for-profit career college sector to the subprime mortgage banking industry is as silly as it is simplistic. In the case of the latter, mortgage broker companies, many that came from nowhere and soon disappeared to the same location, originated loans among many unqualified applicants. The loans were then bundled and sold on securities markets to buyers with little or no knowledge of the underlying paper. Those who were tasked with evaluating the securities ignored their fundamental responsibility. A housing bubble fueled this otherwise illogical and ill-advised series of transactions. In a market producing double-digit year on year annual housing price increases, home buyers had little reason to question their ability to repay loans, brokers had little reason to question the buyers' ability to do so, and investors had little reason to question the integrity of the securitized mortgages. Take away the bubble, and the fantasy of no-risk, widely shared subprime mortgage lending evaporates.

The higher education dynamic is very different. First, there is no bubble to stimulate irrational behavior. No one questions the need to increase the number of students with post-secondary degrees, as it benefits the U.S. economy generally and the students individually. In fact, increasing educational opportunity and solid outcomes is essential to this country's economic future. Most students in career and professional schools use federal loans and grants, but the lent portion must be repaid. The value of the student investment grows over time, but this happens the old fashioned way: students earn it by gaining the credentials and necessary skills, applying those skills in early stage jobs, and climbing the career ladder. And education, as we all know, lasts a lifetime.

## For-Profits Are Accredited

Secondly, the institutions providing the education are not no-name entities, with no future reputation to protect. On the contrary, they are accredited institutions, licensed by the state or states in which they operate, regulated by the Department of Education. Most have a long track record in their respective communities. The accreditors are small, not-for-profit entities, not Wall Street behemoths like those who rated the subprime securities, and had no reason to ask tough questions. The accrediting reviews are done by competitors of the schools they are reviewing, who have every reason to question schools that cut corners, and, in turn, are subject to oversight by the US Department of Education.

Third, unlike subprime mortgage lending where loan underwriting was largely missing in action, career colleges do "rate" prospective students in terms of their chance of success. Contrary to the impression that Mr. Eisman tried hard to create, institutions have little incentive to fill seats with students who cannot succeed academically. For one thing, if the students drop out soon after enrolling, the schools have to return to Uncle Sam any government supplied/backed funds the students received and then used to pay for their education. Nationally accredited colleges and universities must meet specific outcome metrics for retention/graduation and placement to retain accreditation and Title IV program eligibility.

---

*The emergence of the non-traditional student in higher education is one of the great untold stories of the day—a triumph of enlightened public policy leadership.*

---

Beyond accreditation, damage to reputation is also a highly effective check on institutional quality. Career education is a word of mouth business—specially when those words flash around the Internet in milliseconds. Those institutions with shoddy educational offerings, unqualified students or high drop-out rates quickly find themselves enjoying diminishing returns.

Fourth, career colleges have a stake in the success of the student because they themselves are graded on outcome metrics. Failure to achieve specific metrics flunks schools out of the Title IV student aid programs. Mortgage brokers had no such stake in the success of borrowers at home ownership and paid no penalty when buyers defaulted on their home loans. The lenders themselves had little risk because they securitized their loans.

## Higher Education Market Changing

Mr. Eisman correctly notes that the size and significance of career education is growing rapidly, but this is so for reasons that have nothing to do with the irrational exuberance of an overheated market. Just the opposite. The higher education landscape is changing because it must change. For most of its history, higher education has been the domain of the privileged few. While from time to time, the government has made dramatic interventions to provide access to a broader swath of society, such as the Morrill Act of 1862 establishing the land grant colleges and the original GI bill which allowed millions of returning veterans to get a college degree, today's traditional colleges and universities are once again primarily the province of the economic elite. In a global economy and a u-shaped recession, educational elitism is a prescription for disaster. The consequences of not changing, of allowing the American middle class to shrink and the lower classes to grow, are simply untenable.

The emergence of the non-traditional student in higher education is one of the great untold stories of the day—a triumph of enlightened public policy leadership. Over 2.8 million students will attend career colleges this year. They will pursue education in more than 500 fields at over 2,900 accredited institutions. And nearly half of them will do all of this while raising children, because 47 percent of our students are parents. They are on average 28 years old, not immediately embarking on their educational track upon high school completion. Additionally, the majority of these students are the first in their family to pursue higher education. Five percent are veterans.

---

*Career college students are very different from traditional college and university students and the education they require tends to be very different.*

---

Career college students are very different from traditional college and university students and the education they require tends to be very different. In form, career college education is tailored, streamlined, flexible, and outcome oriented. It is designed to meet the needs of working, independent adults. Course schedules are aligned to assure access and availability, and course offerings are often presented in a limited, sequential manner. This means that students do not experience long wait times to enroll in a specific class or program, or worse, they do not waste months or years spinning their wheels in poorly defined or ill-fitting majors. Although classrooms and textbooks play a role, the pedagogy is designed to aid the adult learning process by being immersive, hands-on, practical, informed by area employers and shaped by real-world work requirements.

These are innovative processes and methods delivered to a new type of college student at a time of dramatic change, at a time when effective, outcomes-based education is badly needed by students, employers and communities alike. Federal loans and grants provide access to that education and, by doing so, make an affirmative investment in working class adults, social mobility, and the U.S. economy overall. Mr. Eisman cites what he believes is a traditional relationship between matching means and cost in education. Using his "traditional relationship," we should continue to support the idea of having the poorest neighborhoods generally having the worst in terms of public school facilities and the fewest resources.

## An Elitist Approach to Education

I firmly reject his elitist approach to education, both as a social scientist and as one who personally came from very modest means and was able to advance primarily because of the educational opportunities I received. And I reject it on behalf of the tens of millions of Americans who are willing to work hard to get ahead and who deserve a choice on how best to do so.

Sending economically disadvantaged college students to the lowest cost public colleges, he says, would maximize the return on Title IV grants and loans. One important point Mr. Eisman does not understand is that no one "sends" students anywhere. They have choices, and if they choose to attend a career college over a community college or four year school—or not go to school at all—they are doing so in a very competitive environment.

But even if one did want to "send" low income and working adult students to only the lowest cost schools, that would not maximize outcomes from the viewpoint of students or taxpayers. Students graduate from two year career college programs at three times the rate of community colleges. Private sector schools treat a student as an individual, not a number, and determine what interventions are necessary to make that individual succeed. Community colleges are less successful in dealing with at risk populations because, like the secondary public school system, even with a substantial public subsidy, they are resource constrained and therefore must rationalize educational outlays per student. Far from maximizing every dollar, the government's own data on community college graduation rates suggests that this approach diminishes the individual's higher education opportunity and chances of success.

Mr. Eisman ignores this inconvenient truth and points to the fact that private sector colleges and universities account for about 10 percent of enrollments but over 20 percent of federal grants and loans. Again, this is misleading. By focusing only on Title IV funds, Mr. Eisman obfuscates the fact that not-for-profit schools receive billions of dollars in other government funding. In 2007 alone, federal, state and local governments awarded colleges and universities $142 billion in grants, contracts and appropriations. Private sector schools received only 1% of these funds. On a blended gross basis (i.e. not discounting for loans repaid), private sector schools receive only 6% of government education funding—significantly less than their 10% share of the student total. . . .

Now let's take Mr. Eisman on value: "What do these students get for their education? In many cases, NOT much, not much at all," he claims. Everyone is entitled to his own opinions, but not his own facts. And the facts contradict his assertion. Unlike traditional college counterparts, nationally accredited career colleges must meet certain placement outcomes to remain Title IV eligible. Nationally accredited schools do so at a rate of 70 percent, even in a difficult economy. Career college graduates realize an immediate salary "bump" as a result of their degrees. The median annual earnings of a high school graduate are $30,316. The weighted mean of earnings by education level as distributed among career college completions is $39,546, a difference over high school of $9,230. Assuming a total two-year career college investment of $29,533, the graduate's ROI [return on investment] is 31.25 percent. Students who have programs of study at private sector schools that require post graduation examinations, such as nursing, test just as well as students who graduate from traditional schools.

## Lower Income Students Default More

Mr. Eisman expresses concerns about cohort default rates but in so doing fails to provide the appropriate context and in some cases simply misstates the case. A college education is a significant buffer against unemployment. The current unemployment rate of those with only a high school degree is 6 percent higher than that of those with a baccalaureate degree. Still, the economy has a significant impact on the ability of graduates to repay their student loans. Default rates rise when the economy falters and fall when the economy recovers. As a result, cohort default rates are a significant concern for all institutions, not just career colleges, particularly in an environment marked by 8 percent unemployment for new college graduates.

But the simple fact is, as the Government Accountability Office (GAO), the Congressional watchdog, testified last fall at a House hearing, schools that accept lower income students will have higher default rates—regardless of the school's tax status. The default rate is related to the default risk factors, including student characteristics associated with ability to repay.

The cohort default rate for fiscal year 2007 students at career colleges (referred to as proprietary institutions) was 11 percent compared to 5.9 percent for students at public institutions and 3.7 percent for students at private non-profit institutions. If the reported rates take into account the profile of borrowers and defaulters, the cohort default rates for for-profit students differ only slightly with those of community college students (9.9 percent) and are comparable to students attending Historically Black Colleges and Universities (11.5%), whose student demographics are similar to career colleges. While no level of default is acceptable and the career college sector, in concert with the Department of Education, works to improve default prevention strategies, perspective yields understanding.

The truth is that the overwhelming majority of career college students graduate and repay their student loans. Suppose, however, that efforts to rein in the default rate are unsuccessful and the percentage of defaults continues to climb, say to the Department of Education's projected 21.2 percent rate over ten years. On a $500 billion federal loan volume, that is $106 billion, about one-seventh of the $750 billion the federal government will pay in welfare this year [2010]. Or to consider the converse, 80 percent will repay notwithstanding the fact that these are loans made to the economically disadvantaged, removing many from the welfare rolls. According to the federal Office of Management and Budget (OMB), the repayment rate for federal Title IV student loans has actually been rising sharply for more than a decade and has almost doubled.

Currently, including penalties, interest and fees, the federal government actually collects 122 percent of the total amount of student loans it makes.

Career colleges are better than traditional institutions at retaining and graduating the very students that Mr. Eisman claims he is concerned about: minority students, low-income students, first-generation students and at-risk students. More than half of students attending two-year private sector colleges have at least three risk factors, compared to 39 percent of community colleges students. Four-year career colleges whose student populations are at least 60 percent low income have a much higher graduation rate than their traditional counterparts, 55 percent compared to 39 percent for private non-profit institutions and 31 percent for public institutions.

---

*There are simply no enrollment-driven paydays for admissions personnel nor do career colleges spend inordinate amounts on recruitment activities.*

---

## Career Colleges Are Not Marketing Driven

Mr. Eisman accuses career colleges of being marketing machines masquerading as universities, another audacious claim. His evidence is a single disgruntled employee. There are well over 200,000 employees in the career college sector. There is no excuse for high pressure recruiting tactics. Although the approach to student recruitment in an open admissions environment is likely to be very different than in a very competitive admissions environment, the law says enrollment can be just one factor in incentive compensation. As a result, there are simply no enrollment-driven paydays for admissions personnel nor do career colleges spend inordinate amounts on recruitment activities. Indeed, private for-profit mean marketing costs per enrollment are $2,538 compared to $2,366 for traditional institutions. Another recent study by the GAO finds scant evidence of incentive compensation violations, 32 episodes between 1998 and 2009, and 13 of these pertained to traditional colleges and universities. The limited cases draw lots of attention, but the point is the cases are limited. . . .

Returning to his wrongheaded subprime mortgage analogy, Mr. Eisman says for the investment case against the industry to work requires the government to do something, and the Department of Education needs to do "everything and anything to deal with this industry." What he really means is that for the short sellers to make money, the triad of higher education overseers—Federal and state governments and accreditors—has to make bad policy/enforcement decisions based on anecdotes, not facts. For everyone else, especially the students, bad policy, such as the Department's proposed new regulation on gainful employment, would be a disaster. . . .

---

*Higher education in this country is changing, and the non-traditional student is the change agent.*

---

## Higher Education Is Changing

It can rally as it has done in the past to help new generations of American workers meet the challenges of a changing economy. It can serve as the portal to those who live not only in my zip code, but in every zip code to gain the skills and abilities needed to compete and to add value in an ever more demanding work place. And it can adapt its processes and methods to facilitate postsecondary efficiency and effectiveness by eliminating legacy barriers and philosophical constraints.

Or it can insist on retaining the status quo, continuing to enable a situation in which half of American workers have no college credential, where half of college students never graduate, where educational inputs trump outputs, . . . where higher education itself becomes not the means of upward mobility but the club closed to membership for all but the most academically or economically gifted.

It is no secret that the career education sector is under attack by short sellers, trial lawyers, self-styled consumer advocates, and some traditional academics. Although they should know better, these critics use anecdotes to generalize and to make sweeping condemnations of our sector. They seize on admittedly flawed government data to make the most extreme statistical arguments. They exploit the same small cadre of so-called third party experts to generate critical comments. And they recycle old news to give currency to new allegations. In short, they twist the truth to serve their self-interest.

Can career colleges improve? Yes, and they work every day to do so. After all. They have the "triad" watching them. And Congress. And the GAO. And the media. And the short sellers. And the trial lawyers. But, most importantly, they have their students coming to their schools every day with high expectations about how these schools are going to improve their lives, put them in a better place, provide real return—financial and personal—on their investments. And they better deliver, because these students have choices.

America's non-traditional student, returning to higher education, raising a family, working nights and weekends to make ends meet, does not have time for [classic movie] *Animal House* food fights. Higher education in this country is changing, and the non-traditional student is the change agent. We can stand in the way and be marginalized, or we can change the way we think, talk and act towards the players in higher education; embrace all avenues to a postsecondary education; reject biases that limit our ability to recognize what works.

The way forward seems obvious to me.

# 13

# Low-Income Students Take on Too Much Debt at For-Profit Colleges

*Arnold Mitchem*

*Arnold Mitchem is director of the Council for Opportunity in Education.*

*Public policy has created a situation where for-profit colleges have a financial incentive to recruit low-income students to gain access to the federal loans open to these students. As a result, for-profit institutions target low-income students with overly aggressive marketing techniques. In many cases, low-income students would receive a better education by attending public or independent colleges.*

While I believe that the question asked in the title of this hearing [The Federal Investment in For-Profit Education: Are Students Succeeding?] is an extremely critical one with respect to the federal investment in student aid, in my view, it is a question that must be parsed and expanded. If the Committee is simply questioning whether the federal government is getting an adequate return on aid dollars used by students to attend for-profit schools, I would probably not be the best witness to have been invited.

## Are Low-Income Students Protected?

However, by asking the question of whether students are succeeding, the Committee, in fact, has raised some deeper, related issues. The most central one—and the one I believe I am most qualified to speak on is this: *Do the current laws and regulations governing Federal Student Assistance, particularly student loans, sufficiently protect low-income students vis-à-vis for-profit schools?* This leads to a more basic question that lies at the heart of this congressional inquiry: *Are low-income students adequately protected from assuming inappropriate loan debt to attend for-profit schools?*

And my answer to these two questions is a resounding *NO*.

I began my career in higher education over forty years ago when I was appointed the first director of the Educational Opportunity Program for low-income and minority students at Marquette University. My experience guiding underrepresented students through college was a key motivator during my years at the university. Currently, the Educational Opportunity Program and thousands of other TRIO [Federal outreach and student services programs for disadvantaged students] programs continue to steer low-income, first-generation students towards the most appropriate means of pursuing and financing their postsecondary educations. Yet, I appear before the Committee today on behalf of the millions of other low-income students who have not had the benefit of receiving objective information about colleges. It is these students that we must seek to protect not only from unscrupulous and abusive practices within the for-profit sector, but also from the inequities inherent in the relationship between low-income students and for-profit institutions.

As you may know, the organization that I direct, the Council for Opportunity in Education (or "COE"), represents teachers, counselors and administrators who work with low-income and first-generation students. Before COE issued its statement on for-profits and gainful employment, I consulted with many of these individuals, particularly those working in TRIO's Educational Opportunity Centers, Veterans Upward Bound and Talent Search programs, to gain insight into their perspectives on for-profit institutions. In particular, I wanted to find out from them:

1. Were they often able to recommend a for-profit program as the best fit for their students?

2. If yes, when was there a particularly good fit? If no, why do they seldom recommend for-profit programs?

3. How often did they encounter individuals whom they felt had previously been treated inappropriately by for-profit institutions?

Almost without exception, each of the answers I received indicated that it was rare that they found for-profit programs to be the best fit for the students they counseled. Two reasons emerged. First, almost always, they could identify less expensive, publicly supported alternatives in the same area that would not require the student to assume as high a loan burden. Second, in very many instances, TRIO counselors found that many for-profit admissions counselors were not fully forthcoming and did not distinguish their programs from those offered at other public and independent colleges.

Also, virtually all of these TRIO counselors could identify individuals who had been, in their view, harmed by enrolling in a for-profit program. COE is submitting a number of such examples along with my written testimony.

*There simply are not sufficient safeguards in place to protect low-income students in their interactions with for-profit institutions.*

## The Problem: Marketing Tactics

Many TRIO staff pointed to the marketing techniques of the for-profit institutions as the root cause of this problem. As a result of current federal policy, the playing field for low-income students simply is not level. Unwittingly, we have created an environment in which the for-profit institutions have very good reason (and an exceptional level of resources) to heavily recruit low-income students while many publically supported and independent colleges have neither the financial incentives nor the resources to engage in the same state-of-the art, well-targeted, high-pressure marketing. Now the GAO [Government Accountability Office], and TRIO staff, can point to a number of instances that I would say go beyond "state of the art, well-targeted marketing." But, I would urge this Committee to recognize that even in the absence of unscrupulous or simply greedy behaviors on the part of institutions or individuals, currently there simply are not sufficient safeguards in place to protect low-income students in their interactions with for-profit institutions.

These institutions hold up the promise of a better life—in fact, the promise of the American Dream—to individuals of modest means. In the face of such glossy advertisements and tenacious recruiting tactics, it is, in my view, unrealistic to assume that a majority of first-generation and low-income students—who are tackling higher education on their own—will be able to step back, assemble a team of wise and experienced advisors, and ultimately make the best decisions.

A concern repeatedly raised by TRIO counselors was the difficulties many low-income individuals had distinguishing between the value of a particular program and the value of "college." Families where parents are college graduates might find this hard to understand. But many low-income individuals and families have difficulty distinguishing between a for-profit education and a traditional college experience when both can put "college" in their names and both are "endorsed" by the federal government—which provides financing to facilitate their attendance.

A story of a former serviceman served by one of TRIO's Veterans Upward Bound programs comes to mind. This individual completed 54 credits of a 60 credit associate's degree program at a for-profit "college" before being deployed to Iraq. When he returned home and attempted to enroll in a university, he found that none of those credits were transferable, though he had been assured that they would transfer. Often TRIO-eligible students begin their postsecondary careers at for-profit institutions, assuming that it is a building block in their long-term educational plans. But, too often, their enrollment at these institutions hinders those plans. Debt to the for-profit institution, which prevents transfer of credit; confusion about transferability; and default on student loans after enrollment at a high-cost for-profit institution can each serve to create a dead-end for a student's aspirations.

---

*Many public and independent colleges are offering comparable programs to low-income students at a much lower cost than what is being provided at for-profit institutions.*

---

## Public Colleges Are a Better Choice

Now, when advocates like me raise concerns about for-profit institutions, a distinct line of counterarguments emerges. The first and most pronounced is that for-profits are the only institutions providing access to postsecondary education for many low-income youth and adults. This argument is often raised by individuals from minority communities, like me, who are deeply sensitive to issues of discrimination and access. My problem with this argument is that I believe it is based on inaccurate information. In fact, many public and independent colleges are offering comparable programs to low-income students at a much lower cost than what is being provided at for-profit institutions. Low-income students are simply unaware of the entire range of educational opportunities available to them. At this juncture, I would like to take a brief moment to commend this Committee, which has worked diligently to address this issue through the reauthorization of Talent Search, Educational Opportunity Centers and other postsecondary information programs governed by the Higher Education Act. Your emphasis on ensuring financial literacy in these programs is particularly timely. Similarly, efforts made to provide reasonable, income-based repayment plans for student borrowers are also key.

I think all of us in this room agree that access is critical, but access to what? Mountains of debt? Personal and career success must be the answer to the access question. What we are witnessing at COE is that many low-income and first-generation students are not achieving success after participating in for-profit programs. Instead, we are seeing students who emerge with considerable loan burdens and without the ability to obtain meaningful employment or to transfer the credits earned at for-profit institutions to accredited, publically supported or independent institutions.

---

*There is a moral imperative and a responsibility to ensure that all students, regardless of background, race or income level, are fairly represented in higher education.*

---

Similarly, many who oppose greater controls on for-profit institutions argue simply that freedom in the marketplace is a core value of American institutions, and that to interfere with the right of for-profit institutions to make a profit is inappropriate. To go that route, however, would lead us down a road that too closely parallels the one that played a major role in the recent recession. As we saw in the mortgage and banking industries, lending directed at low-income borrowers that is not closely monitored will, almost without exception, lead to abuse. My greatest fear is that the presence of such abuses in the educational arena will—in the foreseeable future—undermine public support for the entire range of federal financial assistance programs.

## For-Profits Target Low-Income Students

I began this testimony by noting that I had been involved in issues and programs designed to increase college opportunity for low-income youth and adults for over forty years. Throughout these four decades, I have tried to govern my interactions with students by a simple maxim: work so that other people's children have the same range of options that my own children, and now grandchildren, have available to them. Like most African-Americans and Hispanic-Americans, I am extremely wary of a two-tiered system of education whereby one set of institutions is available to individuals with information, guidance and means, and another set is provided for those with less information, little guidance and lower means.

If each of the institutions being examined by this Committee were targeting students from a range of economic backgrounds, the necessity of your work would be lessened. But my experience is that they are not. Many of these institutions purposely target low-income students. I believe that there is a moral imperative and a responsibility to ensure that all students, regardless of background, race or income level, are fairly represented in higher education.

# 14

# Excessive Regulation of Student Debt Will Harm Low-Income Students

## Lanny J. Davis

*Lanny J. Davis is a Washington, DC, attorney and former special counsel to President Bill Clinton. Davis is now a paid advisor to the Coalition for Educational Success, a group composed of several companies that own and operate for-profit higher educational colleges in the United States.*

*The gainful employment regulations sought by the Obama administration Department of Education target for-profit colleges and will hurt the minority and low-income students they serve. Student debt is an issue that needs to be addressed, but it needs to be addressed at all institutions of higher learning, not just at the for-profits.*

Suppose that a conservative Republican Administration, in the middle of high unemployment and an economic slowdown, proposed new regulations that would most hurt lower income people and minority groups and the for-profit colleges and universities that serve them? Can you imagine the cries of outrage from liberal critics, condemning "hard-hearted" Republicans targeting the most vulnerable young people in our society?

Lanny J. Davis, "Education Department's 'Gainful Employment' Proposed Regulations Gone Awry," *The Huffington Post*, September 10, 2010. www.huffingtonpost.com/lanny -davis/does-gainful-employment-p_b_736269.html.

Yet that is exactly what the Department of Education's proposed "gainful employment" regulations would likely do. They are almost exclusively aimed at "for profit" private colleges, which are predominantly comprised of lower income and minority students. Let's be careful about characterizing, as some liberals have done, those schools catering to such vulnerable at-risk students with "open admission" policies as "bad actors" whereas the more selective elitist Harvards and Stanfords with less student loan defaults are deemed "good actors."

This has the uncomfortable look and feel of disparate class and racial treatment—which should make liberals very uncomfortable.

So how to explain the paradox that, in fact, these proposed regulations are being proposed by a progressive Democratic Administration and its strongest proponents are liberal members of congress?

## Three Explanations

There appear to be three explanations—each one less meritorious than the other.

The first is a simple misunderstanding of the facts. For example, liberals supporting these proposed regulations rightly complain about marketing and other abuses. But the fact is, such abuses occur at non-profits and public institutions as well as at for-profits and, in any event, the gainful employment regulation doesn't even address the issue of these abuses (although liberal commentators and editorial writers continue to conflate the two issues).

Moreover, those liberals who cite the excess "cost" of student loan defaults among the lower income and minority students ignore two inconvenient, indisputable facts: first, billions of dollars of taxpayer subsidies that go to non-profits and public colleges are not available to for-profits; and for-profits cost taxpayers substantially less per-student each year than non-profits and public colleges, when the approximately $1 billion of taxes/year paid by for-profits are taken into account.

Second, this is a classic example of overly broad regulations confirming the law of unintended consequences.

---

*It is precisely the profit motive that causes for-profits to offer more flexible, consumer-responsive schedules and courses . . . that are directly responsive to recent changes in the job market.*

---

How overly broad? According to the Department of Education's own data released last month [August 2010], its proposed "gainful employment" regulations are so poorly crafted that if applied to non-profits too (which they currently are not), Harvard Medical School, D.C.'s famous minority school, Howard University, and 93 of 100 Historic Black Colleges in the U.S. would all fail the so called loan repayment test. But, supporters of the regulation say, failing just one-of-two tests won't result in loss of student federal loan eligibility. However, just recently, Iowa Democratic Senator Tom Harkin, one of the strongest proponents of this proposed regulation, suggested that failure of the loan repayment test alone should be enough to bar student loans to those who need them the most.

This is why numerous members of the Congressional Black Caucus have strongly weighed in against these proposed regulations and more and more representatives from minority and blue collar communities are waking up and opposing the proposed regulation.

The third explanation appears a classic example of ideology trumping facts: the instinctive negative reaction of many liberals to the word "profit" when associated with providing education. This seems uncomfortably similar to opposition by most liberals to private "charter" schools within urban public school districts, opposition that seemed increasingly paradoxical as more and more inner city parents supported having the choice of charter schools for their children.

## Any Regulations Should Apply to All

The fact is, it is precisely the profit motive that causes for-profits to offer more flexible, consumer-responsive schedules and courses, such as night classes, online courses, and new curricula that are directly responsive to recent changes in the job market.

Clearly Secretary [of education Arne] Duncan needs to put an amber light on the "Gainful Employment Regulation" as it is presently written. As Harry C. Alford, President and CEO of the National Black Chamber of Commerce wrote recently, "student debt is a national problem, one that must be addressed, but imposing regulations on schools that are effectively educating students is unnecessary."

If any regulation is necessary, then Mr. Duncan owes it to the most vulnerable students who will be disproportionately hurt by the current version to use a scalpel, not a hatchet, and to address the issue of excessive student debt at all higher education institutions—not just at for-profits, but at non-profits and public universities as well.

# 15

# Holding For-Profit Colleges More Accountable Helps Low-Income Students

*Marybeth Gasman*

*Marybeth Gasman is an associate professor of higher education in the Graduate School of Education at the University of Pennsylvania.*

*The Obama administration is correct in its efforts to withhold funding for those for-profit institutions that have low rates of gainful employment of their graduates. Jesse Jackson and others who maintain that this crackdown will hurt poor and minority students disproportionately are wrong. Holding educational institutions accountable for the success of their students is the right thing to do.*

The Obama administration has taken steps to stop federal funding of for-profit institutions that are preparing too few of their students for "gainful employment" and that boast high student-loan default rates. Jesse Jackson and several members of the Black and Hispanic Congressional Caucuses have spoke out against these steps. In a letter to Secretary of Education Arne Duncan, Jackson stated, "I am concerned that the proposed rule casts too broad and too general a brush on many institutions, some of whom are doing an excellent job at serving economically disadvantaged and minority students."

Marybeth Gasman, "Gainful Employment, Jesse Jackson, and For-Profit Institutions," *Chronicle of Higher Education*, September 25, 2010. http://chronicle.com/blogs. Copyright © 2010 by Chronicle of Higher Education, Inc. Reproduced by permission.

Herein lies the problem with Jackson's claim: The institutions that are doing an "excellent job" won't lose funding as their students are much more likely to secure employment by earning useful degrees. In addition, these same students will be more likely to pay back their students loans because they are employed. Jackson and others are worried that low-income, first-generation African-American and Latino college students will lose out on opportunities for a college education if the Obama administration holds for-profits more accountable. In truth, holding these institutions more accountable will help racial and ethnic minorities. It does not serve anyone well— African-Americans, Latinos, Whites, the nation overall—to have a degree that doesn't lead to gainful employment or, worse, is not respected by employers. And in fact, granting degrees that are of low quality sets up a two-tiered system in which racial and ethnic minorities as well as low-income Whites pay the price.

---

*Holding [for-profit] institutions more accountable will help racial and ethnic minorities. It does not serve anyone well ... to have a degree that doesn't lead to gainful employment or, worse, is not respected by employers.*

---

## Pushing for More Access

Instead of critiquing the Obama administration's attempt to raise the quality of education for all students—but especially low-income students who frequent for-profit institutions— Jackson, members of the Black and Hispanic caucuses, and all of us for that matter, need to be pushing for more access and greater degree attainment at colleges and universities that care deeply about the future prospects of their students. We need to pay particular attention to racial and ethnic minorities— not only because it is the right thing to do—but because they are quickly becoming the majority of the population.

If you take a closer look at the outcomes of attendance at for-profit institutions, the Obama administration's actions make sense. For example, according to the National Center for Educational Statistics, default rates measured 4 years after students begin repaying their loans show that students who attended for-profit schools have a higher default rate than those who attended non-profit public and private institutions. Specifically, public institutions have a rate of 7.1 percent, private institutions 6.2 percent and for-profits 19.2 percent. In fairness, although the for-profit sector's rate is higher than that of other sectors, according to Government Accountability Office data, it is still beneath the threshold cut-off rates that disqualify schools from Title IV eligibility.

## Graduation Rates Lower at For-Profits

If we turn our attention to graduation rates, for-profits have lower six-year graduation rates than their non-profit counterparts. For example, according to a recent *Chronicle* [*of Higher Education*] article, 44 percent of students who seek a four-year degree at a for-profit institution graduate. That compares with 54 percent of students attending public four-year colleges and 64 percent enrolled at private, non-profit, four-year colleges. If we look more closely, African-Americans graduate at a rate of 40 percent at for-profit institutions, compared to 45 percent at non-profit colleges and universities. Likewise, Latinos graduate at a rate of 50 percent at non-profits, but only at 46 percent at for-profit institutions.

Of course, higher loan-default rates and lower graduation rates can be explained, in part, by the student population served by for-profit institutions. Research tells us that low-income and first-generation students are more likely to default on their loans and less likely to graduate. Other colleges and universities that serve those populations also struggle with the same issues that for-profits do, but they do not operate with a goal of making a profit.

Although there are for-profit institutions that are graduating racial and ethnic minorities at a commendable rate, anytime you mix making money with education—especially the education of low-income, first-generation, or racial and ethnic minorities—it is vital to have the highest level of accountability measures in place. The Obama administration is doing the right thing by holding institutions that make a profit off of education, as well as those that don't, accountable for providing a quality experience to students and making sure these students graduate with valuable degrees.

# 16

## Student Debt Creates Conditions Much Like Indentured Servitude

*Jeffrey J. Williams*

*Jeffrey J. Williams is the editor of the* Minnesota Review *and a professor in the literary and cultural studies program at Carnegie Mellon University. He is also an editor of the* Norton Anthology of Theory and Criticism.

*Taking out loans to finance a college education has left many young people in a position similar to that of the first Europeans who came to America as indentured servants. Like indentured servants, students who take on massive debt to finance their education are faced with working many years simply to pay off their debt. One of the traditional goals of higher education was to create a pathway to equal opportunity for all. Because students with less family wealth take on more student debt, the current system of financing college education reinforces class and social barriers.*

When we think of the founding of the early colonies, we usually think of the journey to freedom, in particular of the Puritans fleeing religious persecution to settle the Massachusetts Bay Colony. But it was not so for a majority of the first Europeans who immigrated to these shores. "Between one-half and two-thirds of all white immigrants to the British colonies arrived under indenture," according to the economic historian David W. Galenson, a total of three hundred thousand to four hundred thousand people. Indenture was not an isolated practice but a dominant aspect of labor and life in early America. . . .

---

*Student debt applies to those with less family wealth, like indenture, reinforcing class differences.*

---

## Reinforcing Barriers Between Classes

College student-loan debt has revived the spirit of indenture for a sizable proportion of contemporary Americans. It is not a minor threshold that young people entering adult society and work, or those returning to college seeking enhanced credentials, might pass through easily. Because of its unprecedented and escalating amounts, it is a major constraint that looms over the lives of those so contracted, binding individuals for a significant part of their future work lives. Although it has more varied application, less direct effects, and less severe conditions than colonial indenture did (some have less and some greater debt, some attain better incomes) and it does not bind one to a particular job, student debt permeates everyday experience with concern over the monthly chit and encumbers job and life choices. It also takes a page from indenture in the extensive brokerage system it has bred, from which more than four thousand banks take profit. At core, student debt is a labor issue, as colonial indenture was, subsisting off the desire of those less privileged to gain better opportunities and enforcing a control on their future labor. One of the goals of the planners of the modern U.S. university system after the Second World War was to displace what they saw as an aristocracy that had become entrenched at elite schools; instead they promoted equal opportunity in order to build America through its best talent. The rising tide of student debt reinforces rather than dissolves the discriminations of class, counteracting the meritocracy. Finally, I believe that the current system of college debt violates the spirit of American freedom in leading those less privileged to bind their futures.

## Rewriting the Social Contract

In a previous essay, "Debt Education," in the summer 2006 issue of *Dissent*, I detailed the basic facts and figures of student-loan debt, pointed out how it rewrites the social contract from a public entitlement to education to a privatized service, and teased out how it teaches less than humanistic lessons, about education as a consumer good, about higher education as job training rather than intellectual exploration, and about civil society as a commercial market rather than a polis. I also promoted some solutions, notably the U.S. Labor Party's proposal for FreeHigherEd and fortified forms of public service linked with college. Here, I look more seriously at the analogy to indenture. While it might not be as direct or extreme a constraint as indentured servitude, student debt constrains a great many of Americans. It represents a turn in American thought and hope to permit such a constraint on those attempting to gain a franchise in the adult or work world. I also want to promote a relatively little known proposal for relieving some of the most inequitable terms of student debt, "Income Contingent Loans."

Indentured servitude seems a strange and distant historical practice, like debtors' prison. But there are many ways that college student-loan debt revises for the twenty-first century some of its ethos and features:

- *Prevalence.* Student-loan debt is now a prevalent mode of financing higher education, applying to two-thirds of those who attend. If upward of 70 percent of Americans attend college at some point, it applies to half the rising population. Like indenture through the seventeenth century, it has become a common experience of those settling the new technological world of twenty-first-century America, in which we are continually told that we need college degrees to compete globally.

- *Amounts.* Student debt has morphed from relatively small amounts to substantial ones, loosely paralleling the large debt entailed by colonial transport. The average federal loan debt of a graduating senior in 2004 (the most recent year for which statistics are available) was $19,200. Given that tuitions have nearly doubled in the last decade and grants have barely risen, and that debt more than doubled from 1994, when it was $9,000, not to mention from 1984, when it was $2,000, one can assume that the totals will continue to climb. Also consider that, as happens with averages, many people have significantly more than the median—23 percent of borrowers attending private and 14 percent attending public universities have over $30,000 in undergraduate loans. Added to federal loans are charge cards, estimated at $2,169 per student in 2004, quite often used for necessities; private loans, which have quintupled in number since 1996, when 1 percent of students took them, to 5 percent in 2004, and which have risen in total to $17.3 billion in 2005, a disturbingly large portion *in addition to* the $68.6 billion for federal loans; and, for over 60 percent of those continuing their educations, graduate-student debt, which more than doubled in the past decade, to a 2004 median of about $28,000 for those with master's degrees, $45,000 for doctorates, and $68,000 for professional degrees.

- *Length of term.* Student debt is a long-term commitment—fifteen years for standard Stafford guaranteed federal loans. With consolidation or refinancing, the length of term frequently extends to thirty years—in other words, for many returning students or graduate students, until retirement age. It is not a transitory bond, say, of a year for those indentured in England or of early student debtors who might have owed $2,000. To be sure, it is not as concentrated as colonial indenture, but it is lengthier and weighs down a student debtor's future.

- *Transport to work.* Student indebtedness is premised on the idea of transport to a job—the figurative transport over the higher seas of education to attain the shores of credentials deemed necessary for a middle class job. The cost of transport is borne by the laborer, so an individual has to pay for the opportunity to work. Some businesses alleviate debt as a recruiting benefit, but unfortunately they are still relatively few. (Another factor is the precipitous rise in student work hours, as Marc Bousquet's stunning indictment, *How the University Works*, recounts. According to recent statistics, students at public universities work an average of twenty-five hours a week, which tends to lower grades and impede graduation rates. Servitude, for many current students, begins on ship.)

- *Personal contracts.* "Indenture" designates a practice of making contracts before signatures were common (they were torn, the tear analogous to the unique shape of a person's bite, and each party held half, so they could be verified by their match); student debt reinstitutes a system of contracts that bind a rising majority of Americans. Like indenture, the debt is secured not by property, as most loans such as those for cars or houses are, but by the person, obligating his or her future labor. Student-loan debt "financializes" the person, in the phrase of Randy Martin, who diagnoses this strategy as a central one of contemporary venture capital, displacing risk to individuals rather than employers or society. It was also a strategy of colonial indenture.

- *Limited recourse.* Contracts for federal student loans stipulate severe penalties and are virtually unbreakable, forgiven only in death, not bankruptcy, and enforced by severe measures, such as garnishee and other legal sanctions, with little recourse. (In one recent case, the Social Security payment to a person on disability was garnisheed.) In England, indenture was regulated by law, and servants had recourse in court; one of the pernicious aspects of colonial indenture was that there was little recourse in the new colonies.

- *Class.* Student debt applies to those with less family wealth, like indenture, reinforcing class differences. That this would be a practice in imperial Britain, before modern democracy and where classes were rigidly set, is not entirely surprising; it is more disturbing in the United States, where we ostensibly eschew the determining force of class. The one-third without student debt face much different futures, and are more likely to pursue graduate and professional degrees (three-quarters of those receiving doctorates in 2004 had no undergraduate debt, and, according to a 2002 Nellie Mae survey, 40 percent of those not pursuing graduate school attributed their choice to debt). Student debt is digging a class moat in present-day America.

- *Youth.* Student debt incorporates primarily younger people, as indenture did. One of the more troubling aspects of student debt is that often it is the first step down a slope of debt and difficulties. Tamara Draut, in her exposé *Strapped: Why America's 20- and 30-Somethings Can't Get Ahead*, shows how it inaugurates a series of strained conditions, compounded by shrinking job prospects, escalating charge card debt, and historically higher housing payments, whether rent or mortgage, resulting in lessened chances for having a family and establishing a secure and comfortable life. The American Dream, and specifically the post–Second World War dream of equal opportunity opened by higher education, has been curtailed for many of the rising generation.

- *Brokers.* Student debt fuels a financial services system that trades in and profits from contracts of indebted individuals, like the Liverpool merchants, sea captains, and planters trading in contracts of indenture. The lender pays the fare to the college, and thereafter the contracts are circulated among Sallie Mae, Nellie Mae, Citigroup, and four thousand other banks. This system makes a futures market of people and garners immense profit from them. The federally guaranteed student loan program was originally a nonprofit corporation, Sallie Mae, but in 2004 Sallie Mae became a private, for-profit corporation, reporting record profits in its first three years.

---

*Student debt is digging a class moat in present-day America.*

---

- *State policy.* The British crown gave authority to the Virginia Company; the U.S. government authorizes current lending enterprises and, even more lucratively for banks, underwrites their risk in guaranteeing the loans (the Virginia Company received no such largesse and went bankrupt). In the past few years, federal aid has funneled more to loans rather than any other form of aid (52 percent of all federal aid, whereas grants account for 42 percent).

## Student Loan Debt Weakens America

My point in adducing this bill of particulars is not to claim an exact historical correspondence between indentured servitude and student indebtedness. But, as I think these particulars show, it is not just a fanciful analogy either. The shock of the comparison is that it has any resonance at all, and that we permit, through policy and practice, the conscription of those seeking the opportunity of education, especially the young, into a significant bond on their future labor and life. While indenture was more direct and severe, it was the product of a rigidly classed, semi-feudal world; student debt is more flexible, varied in application, and amorphous in effects, a product of the postmodern world, but it revives the spirit of indenture in promulgating class privilege and class subservience. What is most troubling is that it represents a shift in basic political principle. It turns away from the democratic impetus of modern American society. The 1947 Report of the President's Commission on Education, which ushered in the vast expansion of our colleges and universities, emphasized (in bold italics) that "free and universal access to education must be a major goal in American education." Otherwise, the commission warned, "If the ladder of educational opportunity rises high at the doors of some youth and scarcely rises at the doors of others, while at the same time formal education is made a prerequisite to occupational and social advance, then education may become the means, not of eliminating race and class distinctions, but of deepening them." Their goal was not only an abstract one of equality, but also to strengthen the United States, and, by all accounts, American society prospered. Current student debt weakens America, wasting the resource of those impeded from pursuing degrees who otherwise would make excellent doctors or professors or engineers, as well as creating a culture of debt and constraint. . . .

## There Are Viable Solutions

In the past year, there has been more attention to the problem of student-loan debt, but most of the solutions, such as the recent interest rate adjustment for current graduates (so the rates didn't rise when the prime rate increased) or laws forbidding graft to college loan officers, are stopgaps that do not affect the structure and basic terms of the system. The system needs wholesale change. I believe that the best solution is "FreeHigherEd," put forth by the Labor Party. It proposes that the federal government pay tuition for all qualified students at public universities, which would cost around fifty billion dollars a year and which could be paid simply by repealing a portion of the Bush tax cuts or shifting a small portion of the military budget. It would actually jettison a substantial layer of current bureaucracy—of the branches of the federal loan program, of the vast web of banking, and of college financial aid offices—thereby saving a great deal. Like free, universal health care, free higher education should be the goal, and it's not impracticable.

---

*Student debt produces inequality and overtaxes our talent for short-term, private gain.*

---

The next best solution, I believe, is "Income Contingent Loans." Income Contingent Loans, as their name implies, stipulate an adjustable rate of payment according to income. They were first adopted in Australia in 1989, the invention of the educational policy expert Bruce Chapman, and have since been adopted in the United Kingdom. They are currently supported by The Project on Student Debt. Such loans represent a pragmatic compromise between free tuition and the current debtor system. They provide a safety net for those with the most debt but least resources and they stipulate a reasonable scale of payment for those doing better.

One of the most pernicious aspects of the current structure of student-loan debt is that it puts a particular burden on those who have lower incomes, especially at the beginning of their careers, because the repayment schedule is fixed (there are very limited terms of forbearance, capping at four years). For instance, an elementary school teacher with a salary of $23,900 (the 2005 median) who has a debt of $40,000 after her four years at a private college would have to pay about 15 percent or more of her salary, before taxes. After taxes it might be closer to 25 percent, which would make ordinary living expenses difficult. Income Contingent Loans stipulate a minimum threshold below which one does not have to pay—23,242 in Australia in 2002. Income Contingent Loans protect those most at risk. . . .

Although it seems as if it crept up on us, student-loan indebtedness is not an accident but a policy. It is a bad policy, corrupting the goals of higher education. The world we inhabit is a good one if you are in the fortunate third without debt, but not nearly so good if you live under its weight. Student debt produces inequality and overtaxes our talent for short-term, private gain. As a policy, we can and should change it.

# Organizations to Contact

*The editors have compiled the following list of organizations concerned with the issues debated in this book. The descriptions are derived from materials provided by the organizations. All have publications or information available for interested readers. The names, addresses, phone and fax numbers, and e-mail and Internet addresses may change. Be aware that many organizations take several weeks or longer to respond to inquiries, so allow as much time as possible.*

**Association of Private Sector Colleges
and Universities (APSCU)**
1101 Connecticut Ave. NW, Suite 900, Washington, DC   20036
(202) 336-6700 • fax: (202) 336-6828
website: www.apscu.org

The Association of Private Sector Colleges and Universities, with over eighteen hundred members, is a membership organization for the private, postsecondary schools, institutes, colleges, and universities that educate and support the career-oriented sector of higher education. Principal APSCU programs focus on public policy advocacy, sector promotion and research, and professional and business development. APSCU conducts and publishes research and analysis on career education, some of which is available on its website.

**The Brookings Institution**
1775 Massachusetts Ave. NW, Washington, DC   20036-2188
(202) 797-6000 • fax: (202) 797-6004
website: www.brookings.edu

Founded in 1927, the Brookings Institution conducts research and publishes in the fields of government, foreign policy, economics, social sciences, and education. The institution publishes the *Brookings Review* quarterly as well as numerous books and research papers, including the Brookings Policy Brief series.

**Center for Academic Integrity (CAI)**
126 Hardin Hall, Clemson University
Clemson, SC   29634-5138
(864) 656-1293 • fax: (864) 656-2858
e-mail: cai-l@clemson.edu
website: www.academicintegrity.org

CAI is a consortium of over 360 institutions who share with peers and colleagues the center's collective experience and expertise on academic integrity. CAI publishes research, assessment guides, and educational resources.

**Education Resources Information Center (ERIC)**
655 Fifteenth St. NW, Suite 500, Washington, DC   20005
(800) 538-3742
website: www.eric.ed.gov

ERIC is a national information system that provides access to an extensive body of literature on education. Supported by the US Department of Education, it maintains a database of more than 1 million records comprising journal articles, research reports, curriculum and teaching guides, conference papers, and books. It also provides research syntheses, electronic journals, online directories, and reference and referral services on various aspects of education.

**The Heritage Foundation**
214 Massachusetts Ave. NE, Washington, DC   20002-4999
(202) 546-4400 • fax: (202) 546-8328
e-mail: info@heritage.org
website: www.heritage.org

The Heritage Foundation is a conservative public policy research organization that promotes policies that align with the principles of free enterprise, limited government, individual freedom, traditional American values, and a strong national defense. The foundation publishes extensively on higher education in its reports, backgrounder series, webcasts, lectures, and other forms of commentary and analysis.

## The National Center for Public Policy and Higher Education

152 N. Third St., Suite 705, San Jose, California   95112
(408) 271-2699 • fax: (408) 271-2697
e-mail: center@highereducation.org
website: www.highereducation.org

The National Center for Public Policy and Higher Education promotes public policies that enhance Americans' opportunities to pursue education and training beyond high school. The center prepares action-oriented analyses of policy issues facing the states and the nation regarding opportunity and achievement in higher education. The center communicates performance results and key findings to the public; civic, business, and higher education leaders; and state and federal officials.

## National Education Association (NEA)

1201 Sixteenth St. NW, Washington, DC   20036-3290
(202) 833-4000 • fax: (202) 822-7974
website: www.nea.org

The NEA is a professional organization open to employees of public schools, colleges, and universities. The mission of the NEA is to ensure that every student in America, regardless of family income or place of residence, receives a quality education. In pursuing its mission, NEA focuses its resources on improving the quality of teaching, increasing student achievement, and making schools safer and better places to learn. Among the publications of the NEA are *NEA Today* magazine and *Higher Education Advocate*, a newsletter.

## US Department of Education

400 Maryland Ave. SW, Washington, DC   20202
(800) 872-5327
website: www.ed.gov

The US Department of Education is the government agency responsible for education issues in the United States. The mission of the department is to provide equal access to education and promote educational excellence. Among other activities, the department administers Pell Grants and student loan programs. The department publishes a variety of newsletters on specific topics relating to education; publications and reports can be accessed online.

# Bibliography

## Books

Zac Bissonnette
*Debt-Free U: How I Paid for an Outstanding College Education Without Loans, Scholarships, or Mooching Off My Parents.* New York: Portfolio Trade, 2010.

Reyna Gobel
*Graduation Debt: How to Manage Student Loans and Live Your Life.* Hoboken, NJ: Cliff's Notes, 2010.

Lynnette Khalfani
*Zero Debt for College Grads: From Student Loans to Financial Freedom.* New York: Kaplan, 2007.

David J. Light
*Discharging Student Loans in Bankruptcy.* Horsham, PA: LRP, 2005.

Martha Maeda
*How to Wipe Out Your Student Loans and Be Debt Free Fast: Everything You Need to Know Explained Simply.* Ocala, FL: Atlantic, 2009.

Brian O'Connell
*Free Yourself from Student Loan Debt: Get Out from Under Once and for All.* New York: Kaplan, 2004.

Margot A. Schenet et al.
*Pell Grants: Background and Issues.* New York: Novinka Books, 2002.

William G. Tierney and Guilbert C. Hentschke
*New Players, Different Game: Understanding the Rise of For-Profit Colleges and Universities.* Baltimore: Johns Hopkins University Press, 2007.

| US Department of Education | *Your Federal Student Loans: Learn the Basics and Manage Your Debt.* Washington, DC: US Department of Education, Federal Student Aid, 2009. |
| Lydia N. Vedmas, ed. | *Federal Student Loans Revisited.* New York: Novinka Books, 2005. |

## Periodicals and Internet Sources

| Carolyn M. Brown | "Attacking Student Loan Debt," *Black Enterprise*, October 2010. |
| Stephen Burd | "The Subprime Student Loan Racket," *Washington Monthly*, November/December 2009. |
| Lindsey Burke | "Pell Grant Increase Would Not Solve the College Cost Problem," Heritage Foundation WebMemo #3060, November 16, 2010. www.heritage.org. |
| Mona Charen | "Not Just One Terrible Idea, but Two!," Real Clear Politics, March 16, 2010. www.realclearpolitics.com. |
| Michelle Asha Cooper | "Five Myths About Student Loan Delinquency," *Forbes*, May 11, 2011. |
| Mike Elk | "Why Are Progressives Fighting Student-Loan Reform?," *American Prospect*, October 6, 2010. |
| Peter Hannaford | "Obama's Costly Student Loan Takeover," *Human Events*, April 19, 2010. |

Froma Harrop          "Take Student-Loan Companies Off Welfare," *Providence (RI) Journal*, March 28, 2010.

John Hechinger        "For-Profit College Grads Also Earn a Life of Debt," *Bloomberg Businessweek*, January 6, 2011.

Chris Kirkham         "For-Profit Colleges Offer High-Risk Loans to Keep Fed Dollars Flowing, Consumer Group Says," *Huffington Post*, February 2, 2011. www.huffingtonpost.com.

Tamar Lewin           "Student Debt Mounts, Shifting Graduates' Options," *New York Times*, April 11, 2011.

Bob Riha Jr.          "Young People Struggle to Deal with Kiss of Debt," *USA Today*, November 22, 2006.

Michelle Singletary   "Personal Finance Tips for Graduates," *Washington Post*, May 14, 2011.

Kurt Soller           "Majoring in Debt," *Newsweek*, February 17, 2009.

Jim Spencer           "For-Profit Schools Fight to Keep Profits," *Chicago Sun-Times*, February 12, 2011.

# Index